THE 7 SINS OF HIGHLY defective PEOPLE

Rick Ezell

Kregel
Publications

Published by Kregel Publications, a division of Kregel, Inc., P.O. Box 2607, Grand Rapids, MI 49501.

Library of Congress Cataloging-in-Publication Data
Ezell, Rick.
The seven sins of highly defective people / by Rick Ezell.
   p. cm.
Includes bibliographical references.
   1. Deadly sins. I. Title.
BV4626.E97   2003
241'.3—dc22   2003015988
ISBN 0-8254-2531-x

Printed in the United States of America

03 04 05 06 / 5 4 3 2 1

Contents

INTRODUCTION

Recently, I received in the mail a recall notice. It looked like the type of recall notice a person might receive for a defective automobile. But it proved to be much more personal than that. Stamped in big red letters were the words *IMPORTANT RECALL,* under which was written the following:

> The maker of all human beings is recalling all units manufactured, regardless of make or year, due to the serious defect in the primary and central component, the heart. This is due to a malfunction in the original prototype units, resulting in the reproduction of the same defect in all subsequent units. This defect has been technically termed *Subsequential Internal Nonmorality,* more commonly known as SIN, as its primary symptom is a lapse of moral judgment. If one is susceptible to loss of direction, foul vocal emissions, lack of peace and joy, or selfish behavior, then one is inflicted with the defect. The manufacturer, who is neither liable nor at fault for this defect, is providing factory authorized repair and service, free of charge, to correct this SIN defect, at numerous locations throughout the world.

I held the recall notice in disbelief. I knew that for some time I had been afflicted with this malfunction. I questioned if my defect was serious enough to merit immediate attention. Before I laid aside the postcard, I noticed that another word was stamped in big red letters at the bottom: *WARNING*. Under that word was written the following:

> Continuing to operate the human unit without correction voids manufacturer's warranty, exposing owner to dangers and problems too numerous to list, and will result in the human unit being permanently impounded.

Now I was growing uneasy. Did someone know the frailty of my condition? Had I not kept up the appearance that I had my act together? Had someone discovered that I, a pastor and all-around good guy, was—dare I say it—a sinner?

As much as I try to ignore or deny the existence of the defect called sin in my life, it does exist. As much as society wants us to believe that our defect is inconsequential, it isn't. As much as we think that through our own human efforts we can function healthily and normally in spite of our defect, we can't. And, as much as we would like to hide our defect from others, the One to whom it matters the most already knows. We have been found out.

The church fathers of the Middle Ages listed seven sins and called them the "deadly sins." They believed that all other sins grew out of them. They urged people to purge themselves of these sins. What the medieval church fathers knew then, social scientists are now admitting: we are defeated today by these same sins. The seven deadly sins are just as prevalent today as they were in the past. If left unchecked they will not only defeat us, they will destroy us.

The Reasons for the Recall

Sin is serious business. Sin has serious repercussions. Why does God issue the recall regarding our moral defectiveness? Why does God not consider sin a laughing matter? The reasons are twofold.

First, sin contaminates every human being. Every person on God's green earth is infected with it. "For all have sinned and fall short of the glory of God" (Rom. 3:23). The hedonists are infected because they are pleasure centered rather than God centered. The judgmentalists are infected because they are high-minded rather than God-minded. The legalists are infected because they are work driven rather than grace driven. Liberals are infected, but so are fundamentalists, including Baptists. For that matter, so are Methodists and Mormons, Catholics and charismatics, rich and poor, and Americans and Russians. People locked in jail cells and people living in luxury can't escape it. Both laity and clergy are infected.

No one is immune. No one includes me—and you.

Make no mistake about it: sin is real. It is just as real as the air we breathe. Trying to escape it and its effects is like trying to get away from the air we breathe. This condition, this nature, this defect, is a part of each of us.

Sin not only contaminates every human being but also contaminates every part of being human. It is like a drop of dye placed in a clean glass of water; the dye's color permeates every molecule of water. It is like a rotten apple in a bushel basket; the toxins of the rotting apple eventually infect the whole bunch.

Sin is destructive. It contaminates our relationship with God, those we love, and our inner peace and harmony. Tony Campolo states, "Each of us comes into the world with a predisposition to live in such a way as to inflict pain on those who love us most, and to offend the God who cares for us infinitely."[1]

The contaminating nature of sin hinges on the diabolical characteristics and consequences of disobedience and death.

Sin starts with disobedience. First and foremost, sin is disobedience against the will, commands, and nature of God. Sin is more like the act of a traitor than that of a criminal. A criminal violates the law; a traitor violates his citizenship. Sin is far worse than breaking the law. It is breaking the relationship with the Grace-giver. Sin is a raised hand,

---

1. Anthony Campolo, *Seven Deadly Sins* (Wheaton: Victor Books, 1987), 9.

a clenched fist, a blow to the face of God. It is more than doing bad things; it is breaking a relationship.

When one speeds on the highway, he violates traffic laws. When one is offside in a football game, he violates the rules of football. When one sins, he violates the covenant with God. Sin is the only thing that can violate our fellowship with God. That disobedience has damning consequences.

Sin leads to death; it is a fatal disease. It sentences us to a slow, painful death. Sin does to life what shears do to flowers. A cut of the stem separates flowers from the source of life. Cut flowers in a bouquet might look attractive, colorful, and strong. But watch the flowers over time, and the leaves will wilt and the petals will drop. No matter what you do, the flowers will never live again.

When Chinese dictator Mao Zedong died in 1976, his physician, Dr. Li Zhisui, was given an impossible task. Mao's body was to be preserved permanently. So the doctor pumped twenty-two liters of formaldehyde into his body. His faced swelled, his ears stuck out at right angles, and the chemical oozed from his pores.

Don't we try to do the same thing? We don't pump formaldehyde into a corpse, but we do try to pump life into a soul.

Just as dead flowers have no life, a dead body has no life. Humans with sin defects have no spiritual life. Cut off from God, the soul withers and dies. The consequence of sin is not a bad day or a bad mood, but a dead soul. Try as we might to look alive, we are dead in our sins.

Procedures for Authorized Repair

Although sin contaminates every human being and contaminates the being of every human, it is not fatal to be a sinner. Denying that we are sinners, however, is deadly. If unrecognized and unresolved, the sin within will destroy us from without. The sin defects of our being make us wilt, turn brown, lose our luster, and eventually die. We are thrown over to the side of the road to be picked up by a garbage truck. We are robbed of meaning, prevented from being healthy and whole persons, estranged from a loving relationship with God, and destined for eternal damnation.

What do we do?

In his book *Fuzzy Memories*, Jack Handey writes, "There used to be this bully who would demand my lunch money every day. Since I was smaller, I would give it to him. But then I decided to fight back. I started taking karate lessons. But then the karate lesson guy said I had to start paying him five dollars a lesson. So I just went back to paying the bully."[2]

Isn't that most like us? Too many of us feel it is easier to pay the bully than it is to learn how to defeat him. Too many of us keep trying to function with the defect rather than getting it repaired. Too many of us succumb to defeat rather than learn the countermeasures that lead to victory.

This book reveals the offensive strategy that we can take when the enemy attacks. That strategy includes the following action steps.

Recognize sin for its destructive and diabolical nature. Sin violates the covenant relationship with God. It is disobedience against a gracious and loving heavenly Father. Most of us never see the magnitude of our defect because the essence of sin is denial. Each section of this book will first identify and describe the seven deadly sins so that we will recognize the vicious and wicked characteristics of each of them.

Resort to the proper tactics for defeating Satan. We are in a battle with all of the forces of evil. But it is a winnable battle. Fortunately, the Bible provides a workable strategy that will lead to victory over the deadly sins. In our day of unparalleled temptation, every person must know how to overcome Satan. The second chapter in each section will provide a detailed strategy for bringing about each sin's demise.

Release sin through the power of confession. Confession does for the soul what the mechanic does for the defective car. Confession is the act of allowing God to work on our defective lives. Confession is not begging God to forgive us but agreeing with God about the sin defect. God's sin-meter does not lie. It always tells the truth. And there are times when we have to agree with the Father that we are in desperate need of repair and forgiveness.

Confession is owning up to the fact that our behavior wasn't just the result of bad parenting, poor genes, jealous siblings, or a chemical

---

2. Jack Handey, *Fuzzy Memories* (Kansas City: Andrews and McMeel, 1996), n.p.

imbalance. Any or all of those factors might be involved. After all, human beings are complex. But confession means saying that somewhere in the mix was a choice, and we made that choice, and we do not need to excuse it, explain it, or even understand it. Rather, the choice needs to be forgiven. And it is forgiven when we admit to our dishonesty of trying to live on our terms instead of God's. That's where the release comes in.

As you read each section, especially the one dealing with the particular sin that trips you, take time to confess your mistakes and defects. Seek God's forgiveness.

Remove sin from our lives. First there is a *why,* then there is a *how* to removing sin from our lives. The primary reason we want sin removed from our lives is to restore our relationship with our heavenly Father. We are human beings created to be in relationship with God; as long as unconfessed sin exists, however, that relationship will be broken. Second, we will never experience victory in one area of our lives while sin exists in another area. In other words, we can't receive blessings on the one hand while being disobedient on the other hand.

How, then, do we remove sin from our lives? Honestly, we can't. We have neither the strength nor the moral completeness to accomplish such a monumental task. For that, we have to rely on another person, and that other person is none other than Jesus Christ, the Savior of the world. As you read, reflect on Jesus' sacrifice on the Cross, bearing the sins of all humans so that our sins would be removed permanently from our record.

The penalty for sin is death; that's one of the reasons they are called deadly. Someone—either we or a substitute—has to die for our sins. We are given a choice: allow sin to take its course, leading ultimately to death, or trust in Jesus, who died for our sins.

Regardless of whether we realize it, we are in a war. The bombs and bullets of Satan's attacks are all around us. Many people have succumbed to the deadly darts and lie defeated. But we don't have to be victims. We don't have to lose the battles or the war if we employ countermeasures against our enemy. This book is a militant call to employ those countermeasures. They are effective in winning the battle against the seven deadly sins.

THE SIN OF PRIDE

1.

THE PRISON THAT BINDS

Vince Lombardi coached the Green Bay Packers during their glory years of the 1960s. He had a monstrous ego, an unlimited confidence, and an arrogant pride that were not always healthy. All sorts of stories exist about him—some true, some fiction. One story tells of an incident that occurred when he was in a championship playoff. His wife was not able to attend the game for some reason, and that disappointed Vince. No one thought that the Packers were going to win, but, against all odds, they did. You can imagine the coach's exhilaration.

When he came home, his wife was already asleep. He tried to slip into bed without waking her. But when his cold feet touched her legs, she said, "God, your feet are cold." Quick as a flash, Lombardi replied, "When we are in bed, just call me Vince."

I suppose, if we are honest with ourselves, all of us at times think that we are God. Or, at least, we want to be God. We want to exhibit our power, flaunt our egos, seize center stage, and commandeer the throne to control our own little world. To be like God was the original temptation!

Lombardi is not alone. Ramses II, Egyptian monarch of the thirteenth century B.C., ordered mammoth structures built to buttress his huge ego. A ship, larger and more glorious than any ship before it, once sped through a dangerous area of the sea. She had been warned by radiotelegraph of icebergs ahead, but for some reason her crew did not slow down. "God himself," one deck hand had said to a passenger a few days earlier, "could not sink this ship." But the *Titanic* struck an iceberg, and fifteen hundred men, women, and children lost their lives.

The First Sin

The sin of our first parents, Adam and Eve, was the desire to be like God. "You will not surely die," the serpent said to the woman. "For God knows that when you eat of it your eyes will be opened, and *you will be like God*, knowing good and evil" (Gen. 3:4–5, emphasis added). Satan's hook, "You will be like God," had scored its mark. Adam and Eve did eat the fruit, and the rest is, shall we say, sinful history. It was the same hook that brought the fall of Satan from heaven in the first place. Satan said in his heart, "I will ascend to heaven; I will raise my throne above the stars of God; I will sit enthroned on the mount of assembly, on the utmost heights of the sacred mountain. I will ascend above the tops of the clouds; *I will make myself like the Most High*" (Isa. 14:13–14, emphasis added).

There it is—"I will make myself like the Most High"—the same temptation to which Adam and Eve succumbed: "You will be like God." This arrogance infected Vince Lombardi, Ramses II, and the crew of the *Titanic*. And you and I contend with it daily. The Greeks called this arrogance *hubris;* the Bible calls it pride. It is exaggerating our worth and power, overrating our superiority, and possessing unreasonable conceit. Its synonyms are *vanity, conceit, arrogance, egotism, boastfulness, selfishness,* and many more such terms. It has been recognized since ancient times to be a root of cruelty and evil. It produces high-blown, stiff-necked, puffed-up, and stuck-up people.

When we step proudly into God's shoes, we discover that it is a bad fit, just as when a three-year-old tromps around the house in her daddy's shoes—it doesn't work so well. We think it's cute, but to let the child live her life in shoes that are too big would be disastrous.

In his heyday, Muhammad Ali was always proclaiming, "I am the greatest." Once he boarded an airplane and refused to buckle his seat belt. The flight attendant came by and said, "Mr. Ali, you will have to put on your seat belt before we can take off."

"Superman don't need no seat belt," Ali replied.

The flight attendant, weighing no more than a hundred pounds dripping wet, said in her soft voice, "Superman don't need no airplane either."

Before I continue, let me say that not all pride is bad. One can have the pride of a job well done, self-respect, dignity, and the joy of seeing others succeed. The pride that Scripture condemns is the devil's strategy to attack us, not at our weakness but at our strength. Pride is the itch for recognition. It seeks to put our strength on display for the entire world to see. It is the sin expressed in the need to always put "I" at the center. Pride is a swelling of the heart. It eats away at our heart like a cancer, destroying love, contentment, and even common sense.

The Prison of Pride

Buddy Lamar, from my hometown, was a celebrated war hero. While at war, Buddy's fiancé married another man. This rejection broke his heart and his spirit. With no family, when he returned home from the war, he moved into an abandoned house and lived with his dozen cats. He did odd jobs around town. Little happiness existed in his life. I asked my daddy why Buddy was like he was. "Well, I guess the reason is that after his war experience and breakup he thought he didn't need anyone else. His pride wouldn't allow him to ask anyone for help." Then my Daddy said, "There is no greater need than when we think we have no need."

Buddy lived in a prison of his own choosing. In fact, everyone inflicted with the disease of pride lives in a prison—prison of pride. This prison is built with the invisible towers of aloofness, the barbed wire of arrogance, the chain-link fence of conceit, and the walls of vanity. The characteristics of the prisoners are the same. The upper lip is stiff. The chin is stuck up. The chest is puffed up. The heart is hard.

The prison of pride is filled with self-made men and women who are determined to pull themselves up by their own bootstraps even if they land on their backsides. It doesn't matter what they did, or to whom they did it, or where they will end up; it only matters that "I did it my way." They are proud men and women who set themselves apart by setting themselves up. But they fail to realize that the person who gets too big for his britches will be exposed in the end.

We see the prisoners all of the time. Like Buddy Lamar, it is the recluse who retreats from the world. Or it is the alcoholic who won't admit his drinking problem. Or it is the woman who refuses to talk to anyone about her fears. Or it is the businessman who adamantly rejects help, even when his dreams are falling apart. Or it is the status-seeking suburbanite who is more concerned about his image than his kid's college education.

Perhaps to see such a prisoner all you have to do is look in the mirror.

Although it is easier to see pride in others, unfortunately, pride is difficult to see in ourselves. But when it raises its ugly head, its destructive power causes great damage.

The Problem with Pride

The Scripture says, "Pride goes before destruction, a haughty spirit before a fall" (Prov. 16:18). We would do well to learn that verse by heart and to heed its warning.

Once a spider built his web in a barn, high up among the rafters, where he started by spinning a long, thin thread attached to the end of one of the beams. With this thread still attached to him, the spider jumped off the beam and spun out more thread on the way down, until he reached the place he planned as the center of his web. From the center he then spun out other threads like the spokes of a wheel, attaching each of them to the walls and other places. Finally, he had an exquisite web that helped him catch many fine, tasty flies. But he grew fat and lazy and vain. (Pride leads quickly to other deadly sins, in this case, gluttony and sloth.)

One day, he was admiring the web that he had spun, and he noticed the long, fine thread that he had first spun from the top beam and said, "I wonder what that is for? I can't imagine why I ever put it there—it doesn't catch any flies." And so on a sudden impulse he broke it. As a result the whole wonderful web collapsed. The spider had forgotten that the one thread—the link to the strongest beam above—supported the whole web.

Such is the individual who thinks that he is God. He or she breaks the vital links to healthy life—both now and forever.

Consider two American leaders. The first led men in the military and became a high-ranking general. His name was Douglas MacArthur. In his book *American Caesar,* William Manchester wrote about MacArthur, "He had the strength and power, he meant to bear rule over others, and he expected tributes from them. . . . This yearning for adulation was his great flaw . . . But it was his manifest self-regard, his complete lack of humility, which lay like a deep fissure at his very core. In the end it split wide open and destroyed him."[1]

The second man led the American people in its highest office. His name was Richard Nixon. In his book *A Time to Heal,* former President Gerald Ford, who also served as Nixon's vice president, pointed out that Nixon "had a brilliant mind, a great sensitivity to the public's political mood and a unique ability to analyze foreign-policy issues and to act decisively on them."[2] He had many qualities necessary to make a great president. But he also had a great weakness. President Ford said of him, "Most of us have hidden flaws or personality quirks that seldom come to the surface. . . . In Nixon's case, that flaw was pride. A terribly proud man, he detested weaknesses in other people."[3] In the end, it was that pride, that unwillingness to recognize and acknowledge his own mistakes in the Watergate affair, that led to his downfall.

Nixon had not known about the break-in at The Watergate beforehand. He found out shortly after it happened. "And I could see why he

---

1. William Manchester, *American Caesar* (New York: Dell Publishing, 1978), 23.
2. Gerald Ford, *A Time to Heal* (New York: Harper & Row, 1979), 34.
3. Ibid., 35.

felt trapped. Some of the people involved . . . were friends of his, and he didn't want to force them to pay the consequences. His pride was stronger than his recognition that he had made a mistake. He viewed admitting the truth in this matter as a sign of weakness, and that was another mistake."[4]

Pride sustains our sinning. The flaws of MacArthur and Nixon remind us that pride makes us worry too much about image and status and what others think of us. It forces us to compare ourselves with others, to always ensure that we have more or better than our neighbor. It persuades us to believe that we deserve better than we have, even to be better than we are, and to pull down whatever we perceive to be superior to us. It prompts us to display an arrogant attitude. It causes us to use others, even dehumanize them. It is the sustainer of our sins and the reinforcer of our motives.

Pride prevents growth. It prompts us to neglect the links with others that would mature us. For example, the person with marriage problems who won't talk about it with anyone else is teetering on disaster. The person with financial woes who won't ask someone for advice is asking for trouble. The person with emotional needs who won't seek assistance will fall deeper into the vortex of despair. Pride prevents them from taking the necessary steps to wholeness and health.

Pride distorts judgment. It causes us to look past common sense, to think that we can be more than human. It forces us to work beyond our limits, to attempt activities beyond our capabilities, and to move beyond the boundaries of safe behavior.

Consider another event in Richard Nixon's life. When Nixon was vice president and running for president against Senator John Kennedy, he was warned not to accept Kennedy's challenge to a televised debate. After all, Nixon was the vice president and was far better known than Kennedy, a junior senator. But Nixon took great pride in his debating skills. He campaigned strenuously until the last minute. When eighty million Americans turned on their television sets, they saw a marked contrast between the two men. Kennedy looked fresh, tanned,

---

4. Ibid., 35–36.

and vibrant; Nixon looked surly, unshaven, and baggy eyed. The debate was a major victory for Kennedy.

Kennedy, of course, went on to win the presidency by a slim percentage. Most analysts agree that if not for the debacle of the televised debate, Nixon would have won the election. But pride clouded Nixon's judgment. And the rest, as we say, is history.

Pride destroys relationships. It severs the links with others that would build community. When the heart is filled with its own self-preoccupation and self-pleasure, no room is left for others. Having no room for others increases our solitude, and we become more and more alone. Convinced of our own abilities and self-sufficiency, we deny that we need community. Even more tragically for others, we refuse to meet the obligations of being in community.

Pride separates us from God. It cuts off the most vital link of all—the link with our heavenly Father. Pride's most destructive work makes it difficult for us to accept the free gift of salvation. Full of ourselves, thinking that everything is earned, we walk away from the most important relationship of all. D. L. Moody was right, "God sends no one away empty except those who are full of themselves."[5]

Never underestimate the destructive consequences of pride.

The myth of Daedalus describes a boy, Icarus, who, with his father, was imprisoned by the king in a large maze on an island. "The king may control the land and sea," Daedalus told his son, "but not the regions of the air." So the inventor-father built two pairs of wings, one for himself and one for his son. Just before they took off to freedom, the father warned his son to fly at a moderate altitude or the sun would melt the wax that held the feathers fast. As they flew away from the island, the new-found power and freedom went to the boy's head, and he began to fly higher and higher.

As Icarus climbed in exaltation, the heat of the sun melted the wax, and the wings fell apart. He plummeted to the sea, thrashed about and began to sink, the waters closing in over him.

---

5. Cited in Bruce H. Wilkinson, *30 Days to Experiencing Spiritual Breakthroughs* (Sisters, Ore.: Multnomah Publishers, 1999), 68.

The fictional Icarus met his death largely because of his pride. So the next time you find your head in the clouds thinking that you are God, know that you won't be there long. You, too, will be brought low. You will find the waters entombing you.

But there is hope. And there is help. There is a way to break out of the prison of pride. When we take that road, we not only discover freedom but also encounter God.

Study Questions

1. In what areas of your life do you most struggle with pride?

2. Contrast "good" pride with "bad" pride. What are the positive and negative traits of each?

3. In what ways does our culture elevate the image of the self-made man and woman, thus feeding the destructive nature of pride?

4. Reflect on D. L. Moody's observation, "God sends no one away empty except those who are full of themselves." What are the implications of that statement?

5. What are three action steps you could take immediately to break the chains of pride imprisoning you?

2.

SECURING THE RELEASE

"God's Little Workshop" was the name of George Washington Carver's busy laboratory in which the famous scientist pursued his quest for knowledge. There in his lab he asked in prayer to discover the uses of what was then a lowly, unesteemed crop: the peanut.

"Dear Mr. Creator," the humble man began, "please tell me what the universe was made for?"

"Ask for something more in keeping with that little mind of yours," God answered. So Mr. Carver tried again.

"Dear Mr. Creator, what was man made for?"

Again the Lord replied, "Little man, you ask too much. Cut down the extent of your request and improve the intent." So the scientist tried once more.

"Then, Mr. Creator, will you tell me why the peanut was made?"

"That's better," the Lord said, and, beginning that day, Carver discovered more than three hundred uses for the lowly peanut.

Because George Washington Carver was able to admit the limits of his understanding, God was able to open the doors of discovery to him. In fact, Mr. Carver's humility was as famous throughout America as his brilliance.

George Washington Carver's humble attitude stands in sharp

contrast to a world that says, "Promote yourself, advance your cause, and push your own agenda even at the expense of others." In our day of plenty, multitudes of people spend a lifetime ascending ladders, grasping and groping for more and more.

While the world calls for upward mobility, the Bible speaks of downward mobility. The world says that one ascends into greatness. As evidenced by George Washington Carver's example, however, the Bible reveals that one descends into greatness. The world thrives on pride. The Bible leads us in a different direction, toward a different attitude.

The Way Up Is Down

The word for this topsy-turvy attitude is humility. The way up is down. This is perhaps the most counterculture virtue in all of Scripture, especially for people who are grasping for the top. Simply stated, the message of humility is that if you want to be truly great, then the direction you must go is down. The way to find release from pride and become great in God's eyes is through humility. This path of downward mobility is not simply the best of many options to break the chains of pride. It is the *only* route.

In a collection of children's letters to God, Wayne, age eleven, wrote, "Dear God, my dad thinks he is you. Please straighten him out."

We all need straightening out—for our own good. In the New Testament book of James is written, "God opposes the proud but gives grace to the humble" (James 4:6). We have to escape the walls of our lofty prison and meet God on the soil of humility. It is worth remembering that the root of the words *humiliation* and *humility* is *humus*, meaning dirt or soil. We meet God more often in the manure of failure than on the mountain of success, and more often on our knees begging for mercy than on our toes grasping for more.

Humility is not self-hatred or lack of self-confidence. Neither does it imply that a person becomes the proverbial doormat, allowing everyone he encounters to walk all over him. Nor does a humble person look down on themselves or their abilities. Furthermore, humility is not a call to mediocrity and a substandard quality of life. Humility, as evidenced by George Washington Carver, is thinking true and realistic thoughts about God and ourselves. It is the habitual quality whereby we live in the truth: we are creatures and not the Creator, our lives are a composite of good and evil, and in our littleness we have been given extravagant dignity.

A humble person increasingly sees himself or herself as he or she really is: "wretched, pitiful, poor, blind and naked" (Rev. 3:17). We are flawed. We sin. We miss the mark of God's glorious ideal. We are needy, incomplete, and inadequate in ourselves. We are total dependents. We are fallen creatures in need of help to get up so we can become all that God desires.

Like two sides of the same coin, a humble person sees not only himself as he is but also God as he really is—majestic, sovereign, omnipotent, and gracious. We see him as a God of tender love and mercy who cares deeply about us and longs for an intimate relationship with us. We see a God who went to extreme measures to communicate his love and reach us in our frailty. We witness a God who ". . . made himself nothing, taking the very nature of a servant, being made in human likeness. And being found in appearance as a man, he humbled himself and became obedient to death" (Phil. 2:7–8). From power to powerlessness, from the pinnacle of heaven to the poverty of this earth, from a glorious crown to an old rugged cross, from glory to the grave, from divinity to death. Jesus did not reach down from the sanctity of heaven, mind you, but reached out, standing on the dirt of earth as a lowly servant. God's descent to this world is the epitome of humility.

Pride, the antithesis of humility, is a spiritual cancer that eats away at our spiritual eyes, rendering us blind. In a circular way, pride makes us blind to the sin of pride in our lives. In a demonic catch-22, pride causes us to chase our spiritual tails. We cannot see our pride because we are so full of it. Pride is the spiritual veil that blinds us to the truth about ourselves and obscures our need for God. This is why so many people reject Jesus. They do not come to him because they think that they have no need for him. Their pride blinds them to their desperate need for a savior and to their own sinfulness.

Pride metastasizes into something more dreadful. It is the cancerous root of most vice. Instead of contrition, pride leads to self-righteousness, the thinking that one is like God. Humility, on the other hand, always morphs into something more beautiful; it is the fountainhead of the other virtues. It is what we need. How do we get it?

Steps to Humility

Most of us have been kidded at one time or another about our lack of humility. People will say, "Didn't you write the book *Humility and How I Obtained It?*" Usually, if we are humble, we don't realize it. The moment we consider ourselves humble, we are surely wrong. We become proud of our humility and therefore lose it. So humility is more of a process than a destination. Following are some of the steps to take on the road to humility.

Become aware of pride. The tempter, who himself was seduced by pride, always appeals to our human inclinations and desires. He always makes attractive offers that blind us to the subtle forms of pride. He knows that we frail humans have difficulty recognizing pride as sin when it is held up as a virtue. Athletes are extolled for having pride in their performance. We talk of taking pride in craftsmanship. Pride is rewarded in business and industry.

Although it is difficult to spot in most areas of life, pride is easier to detect in the relational dimension of our lives. We constantly are comparing ourselves to those who are a little lower on the ladder of success or are not as far down the road of achievement as we are or who do not live in the neighborhood of our fancier homes.

Humility is the opposite attitude. Former President Harry Truman used to say, "I was here by accident and I try to remember where I came from and where I'm going back to." We would do well to remember that, too.

Before, we proceed, let's remember that an awareness of pride is the first step to humility. Let's not despair of the many facets of this sin in our lives but rather use our knowledge of it as an opportunity for growth.

Dispel the myth. A myth has circulated for years. It sounds spiritual. Some people, unknowingly, have said that it is from the Scripture, but it is a lie. That myth is that "God helps those who help themselves." Nothing could be further from the truth. The reality is that God helps those who *can't* help themselves. Sometimes it takes a tragedy or a crisis before we realize that we aren't in control or sovereign. That is where pride—the feeling that one is God—is so destructive. As long as we think that we are on the throne, in control, above everyone else, we will never see our need to humble ourselves before God.

Humble people see their need for God. The proud do not see that need. In Dante's *Inferno,* the proud are punished by having to carry a huge stone that bends them double, so they cannot lift their eyes from the ground. Those who looked down on everyone else in their lives are now unable to look up at God or anything else.

Two brothers grew up on a farm. One went away to college to make a name for himself. He earned a law degree and quickly became a partner in a prominent law firm in the state capital. The other brother stayed on the family farm.

One day, the ambitious lawyer came and visited his brother, the farmer. Pompously, he asked, "Why don't you go out and make a name for yourself? Why don't you be somebody in this world so you can hold your head up high like me?"

The other brother pointed and said, "See that field of wheat out there? Look closely. Do you see it?"

"Yeah, what about it?"

"Notice carefully that those heads that are most mature and well filled bend low to the ground. Only the empty heads stand up tall."

The point is clear: empty heads stand tallest; mature hearts bend down low before God. We are never more like the devil than when we are trying to elevate ourselves. And we are never more like Jesus than when we humble ourselves.

Allow God to work. In Nikos Kazantzakis's novel *Christ Recrucified* is a scene in which four village men confess their sins to one another in the presence of the pope. One of the men, Michelis, cries out, "How can God let us live on the earth? Why doesn't he kill us to purify creation?"

"Because, Michelis," the pope answered, "God is a potter; he works in mud."[1]

The pope could have said that God works *only* in mud. Those who try proudly to lift themselves out of the mud by their own efforts only frustrate the work of the Artist.

The grace of God, which precedes everything else, proclaims that God lifts graciously those who cannot lift themselves. "God opposes the proud but gives grace to the humble. . . . Humble yourselves before the Lord, and he will lift you up" (James 4:6, 10). The humble qualify for God's grace.

When we're humble, God is free to lavish his grace upon us, to fill our lives with special favors, and to work beyond compare. As we humble ourselves, his Spirit leads us into an ever-growing enjoyment of the spiritual benefits that we have in Christ. If we fail to humble ourselves, we miss his work and expose ourselves to his chastening.

Follow God's lead. The humble will always have God as their guide. We can't go wrong following God's lead. Jesus was brought low. He humbled himself, even to death. But his story does not end on the Cross. At the Cross, the descent was complete. But that was Friday; Sunday was coming. And on Sunday, Jesus was resurrected to life. The ascent commenced. And "God exalted him to the highest place" (Phil. 2:9).

The journey of Jesus reveals some powerful lessons. Only in giving do we receive. Only in losing do we win. Only in dying do we live. Only in humility are we exalted.

In *Guideposts,* Ronald Pinkerton described a near accident he had while hang gliding. He had launched his hang glider and been forcefully lifted 4,200 feet into the air. As he was descending, he was hit suddenly by a powerful new blast of air that sent his hang glider plummeting toward the ground.

---

1. Nikos Kazantzakis, *Christ Recrucified* (Oxford: Bruno Cassirer, 1966), 186–87.

I was falling at an alarming rate. Trapped in an airborne rip-tide, I was going to crash! Then I saw him—a red-tailed hawk. He was six feet off my right wingtip, fighting the same gust I was. . . .

I looked down: 300 feet from the ground and still falling. The trees below seemed like menacing pikes.

I looked at the hawk again. Suddenly he banked and flew straight downwind. Downwind! If the right air is anywhere, it's upwind! The hawk was committing suicide.

Two hundred feet. From nowhere the thought entered my mind: *Follow the hawk.* It went against everything I knew about flying. But now all my knowledge was useless. I was at the mercy of the wind. I followed the hawk.

One hundred feet. Suddenly the hawk gained altitude. For a split second I seemed to be suspended motionless in space. Then a warm surge of air started pushing the glider upward. I was stunned. Nothing I knew as a pilot could explain this phenomenon. But it was true: I was rising.[2]

We all have had similar downturns in our lives, reversals of fortunes, humiliating experiences. We want to lift ourselves up, but God's example, like the red-tailed hawk, tells us to do just the opposite. God's Word tells us to dive, to humble ourselves under the hand of God. If we follow his lead, God will send a thermal wind that will lift us up.

In the end, if we are willing to follow his lead and allow him to work, if we are willing to humble ourselves, then, like Mr. Carver, we'll learn to appreciate the lowly "peanuts" of our experience that are dug up from the soil of our lives. In "God's Little Workshop" we will discover, as he did, a life of grace and bounty.

On the other hand, if we choose to go it alone, if we are not yet ready to be humbled, one day we will be. If we are on God's throne, we will be knocked off. We will lose control. We will be brought low. We will realize that we are not God. And when we find ourselves in the

---

2. Ronald Pinkerton, *Guideposts,* September 1988.

dirt, the mud, and the manure of failure, we should call out to God. He'll be ready then to lift us up and set us free from our prison of pride.

Study Questions

1. What immediately comes to your mind when you hear the word *humility*?

2. Cite some biblical examples of "downward mobility."

3. Why is the path of downward mobility the only route to breaking the chains of pride?

4. Reflect on the myth: "God helps those who help themselves." Why is it such a vicious lie?

5. Compare and contrast the connection between grace and humility.

6. In what ways do you need to follow God's lead of humility?

THE SIN OF ENVY

THE SIN OF THE
EVIL EYE

It's been called "the green sickness," "a torment," and "the most corroding of the vices." Philip Bailey vividly described it as "a coal come hissing hot from hell."[1] The *it* is envy.

And, speaking of hell, no one has done a better job of portraying envy than Dante. In his *Purgatory,* the envious sit like blind beggars by a wall. Their eyelids are sewn shut. The symbolism is apt, showing the reader that envy is a blinding sin—partly because it is unreasonable and partly because the envious person is sewn up in himself. Swollen with poisonous thoughts in a dark, constricting world of almost unendurable self-imposed anguish.

Envy is the sin of the evil eye. The word *envy* is from the Latin *invidia,* meaning "to look maliciously upon." It's to look upon another person with evil intent. It always sees and desires what it does not have. Unlike jealousy, which focuses on possessing what you desire, envy focuses on taking something that you desire from the person

---

1. Cited in Rebecca Davis and Susan Mesner, eds., *The Treasury of Religious and Spiritual Quotations* (Pleasantville, N.Y.: The Reader's Digest Association, 1994), 158.

who owns it. Envy is not just wanting what the other person has; envy wants the other person *not* to have it.

Viewing sin from a biblical chronology, envy is the second of the deadly sins. Pride was first, leading to Adam and Eve's expulsion from the garden because they wanted to be like God. Envy came next, resulting in Cain's murder of his brother Abel. Yet, he wasn't the last in a long line of biblical characters who were afflicted with envy. Envy caused Joseph's brothers to sell him into slavery, it caused Daniel's associates to throw him into the lion's den, and it caused Christ's countrymen to put him on trial. And it caused Saul to be filled with the raging intent to kill his competition as he looked at David through the envious eyes of the green-eyed monster.

Check out the story. David had proven himself a worthy warrior. He prospered. He was victorious. The people appreciated him. They sang songs about him: "Saul has slain his thousands, and David his tens of thousands" (1 Sam. 18:7). Upon hearing this, "Saul was very angry; this refrain galled him. 'They have credited David with tens of thousands.... What more can he get but the kingdom?' And from that time on Saul kept a jealous eye on David" (vv. 8–9).

There's the look—the eye of envy. Saul's envy grew; his eye became so evil that he sought to kill David. If he couldn't be as valiant a warrior as David, then he would erase his competition.

Remember Tonya Harding? She's the Olympic ice-skater who had her competition, Nancy Kerrigan, clubbed on the knee.

That's just like envy. Envy is sort of greed with a vengeance. If greed wants what's out there, envy feels a sense of entitlement to what's inside. When greed and gluttony want something, they grab it and consume it; pride says that if it can't have it, then it isn't worth having. Envy is destined to be perpetually in a state of longing, howling for what seems to be just out of reach like a dog howling at the moon. Greed wants money, pride wants fame, and gluttony wants satisfaction, but envy wants above all to breed more envy. Envy loves wealthy people to go broke, it loves for healthy people to become sick, and it loves for skinny people to grow fat.

Envy's Nature

Envy is the one vice that everybody has experienced. Some people aren't gluttons, others aren't greedy, and even some aren't particularly proud. But everybody has been envious at one time or another. Our human nature has a built-in instinct to be envious. Although we think that envy is often justified and treated as a mild sin, it, too, can be just as deadly as any other sin.

Envy is directed toward people close to us, not toward those who are distant. Note that Joseph's brothers sold him to slavery, Daniel's work associates ratted on him, and Jesus' countrymen turned him over to Herod. And Saul, the king of Israel, was envious of David, the successor to the throne.

Envy seems always to be the sin against those closest to us. It grows naturally in relationships between people who are equals. Two people of the same age and similar interests feel envy most keenly. Doctors envy doctors. Lawyers envy lawyers. Preachers envy preachers. Neighbors envy neighbors. Managers envy managers. Salespersons envy salespersons. One is more apt to envy another of equal standing and status.

The story is told of some demons who were trying to tempt a monk. They thought that a big parish would cause him to be filled with pride. That didn't work. They tempted him with lust by bringing a willing and beautiful young woman into his life. That didn't work. The devil watched their failure and then stepped in to give them a lesson: "Permit me to show you how it is done." He whispered to the holy man, "Your brother was just made bishop of Alexandria." An incredible scowl of envy came over the monk's face, and his whole demeanor drooped. "That," said the devil to the demons, "is what I recommend."

The closer a situation comes to matching your own identity, the higher the stakes become and the more likely envy is to erupt.

Envy reaches for what is out of reach. My family picks apples at an orchard every fall. On one of those excursions, I noticed that I was always looking for the one seemingly perfect apple that was always just out of reach. Although plenty of beautiful apples were well within my reach, it was always the one that was just out of my reach that caught my eye. Such is envy.

Envious people cannot be content that they are victorious and prosperous. All that they can see are others who have received more victories and achieved more prosperity.

You've heard the saying, "The grass is greener on the other side of the fence." Why do we believe that statement? Simple. The grass on the other side of the fence is always out of reach. What is out there, or over there, or beyond what we have is what we want. We envy it.

Envy creates the sense that life is passing one by. The envious often think that they are in their twilight years when the rookie comes to camp, be that a neighbor who drives up with a new SUV or takes off on an exotic vacation to Italy or has a more productive vegetable garden, or a work associate who gets promoted over you or gets a perk that you wanted. Other people might be glad and rejoice with those people, but the envious seethe and become angry.

Envious people often feel a deep disappointment in themselves for not living up to their potential. They think that they ought to get more out of themselves. They go to the twenty-year high school reunion and see a classmate who was behind them in class rank who is now the president of a large company, or one who sat on the bench while they played first team who is making a fortune in real estate, or one who wasn't apart of the "in crowd" at school who now travels the world with her job. They feel a pang of near hatred toward that person. The other people's successes remind them that they are not living their own life to the fullest. They feel diminished by other people's good fortune. And that, in turn, makes them green with envy.

Envy is rotten to the core. The proverb says, "A heart at peace gives life to the body, but envy rots the bones" (Prov. 14:30). Chaucer's Parson reminds us that envy is a foul sin because it sneers against all virtues and against all goodness. Envy is like a little worm inside an apple—it eats us up internally. Much of the non-clinical depression that people experience today is nothing more than internalized envy. Like rust eating iron, envy corrupts men and women.

Envy has within itself its own destructive seed. A man in ancient Greece

killed himself through envy. A city erected a statue to honor the champion athlete in its public games. This athlete had an arch rival who was
so envious that he pledged to destroy the statue. Each night, under the
cover of darkness, he went to the statue and chiseled at its base, hoping
to make it fall. Finally, he achieved his goal and toppled the statue. But
his envy had driven him to the destruction of not only the statue but
also himself because when the statue fell, it fell on him.

The Greek proverb is correct: "Envy slays itself by its own arrows."[2]

Envy is deadly because it will not let us live happily. It robs us of joy.
It will not let us be satisfied with what we have or be grateful for our
talents and personal qualities. It becomes a barrier to the celebration
of who we are. It cheats us of blessings.

When Envy Creeps In

How can we overcome envy? How can we remain calm in the midst
of a competitive society? There is help and hope. The next time envy
creeps into your heart and mind do the following.

Acknowledge envy as sin. Many people struggle with envy for years,
yet never acknowledge its true character: envy is sin. The envious person is not just a victim; he or she bears responsibility. The Scripture
says, "For where you have envy . . . there you find disorder and every
evil practice" (James 3:16). The failure to confess envy will lead to
only more sin. Envy causes conflict with others, travels with its cousin
anger, leads to depression, manifests itself in gossip, and can even pull
the trigger on murder.

Resist comparing yourself with others. "We do not dare to classify or
compare ourselves . . . [it is] not wise" (2 Cor. 10:12). Envious people
are always comparing themselves to others. One way to bolster their
own poor self-esteem is by finding fault with others. But when we
compare ourselves with others, two things happen and both are
destructive. One, when we compare our strength to another person's

---

2. Cited in Solomon Schimmel, *The Seven Deadly Sins* (New York: Oxford University Press, 1997), 60.

weakness, we become proud. Two, when we compare our weakness to another person's strength, we become envious. Either way, we lose.

Recognize God's goodness. In other words, we need to be grateful for what we already have. A myth has circulated since the beginning of time: I must have more than you to be happy. And you must have more than me to be happy. Instead of focusing on what we *don't* have, we need to remind ourselves what we *do* have, giving thanks for God's graciousness in our lives. Do you have life? Health? A job? A house? Clothes? Friends? When we understand God's goodness in our lives, comparisons are meaningless.

Respond to others in love. "[Love] does not envy" (1 Cor. 13:4). When we love other people, we appreciate their strengths and their gifts. We acknowledge that God loves them just as he loves us—no more, no less. And when we choose to love, envy is eradicated from our lives.

Refocus on God. "Don't be envious of sinful people; let reverence for the Lord be the concern of your life. If it is, you have a bright future" (Prov. 23:17 GNB). Only three things will last for eternity—God, His Word, and His people. Not houses, or cars, or jobs, or vacations, or clothes. When we look at people and their achievements and possessions, we need to look at the long haul, not the short term. When I focus on God, my neighbor's achievements and advancements don't matter.

A Hard Price to Pay

One person who did not follow these steps was Antonio Salieri, the court musician to the emperor Joseph of Austria in Vienna. Antonio had dedicated himself to serving God. His only goal was to bring glory to God through his music. All of his life, he dreamed that his music would inspire people toward heaven. He prayed that God would enable him to compose music that would stir people's souls and cause the angels to sing. Unfortunately, Antonio was not blessed with those gifts. His music was pleasant and enjoyable, and his listeners were always entertained, but his compositions were not masterpieces.

Then Antonio met Wolfgang Amadeus Mozart. Antonio became painfully aware of his mediocrity.

Young Mozart was crude, childish, obscene, and lewd. Yet, he was obviously blessed with extraordinary talent. He was a virtuoso on the harpsichord, dazzling everyone who heard him play. His music was intricate, poignant, thrilling, and illustrative at every turn.

Although Antonio was very popular, he recognized that his talent was ordinary and that most of his work would not be remembered. As Mozart's fame grew, so did Antonio's envy. He coveted Mozart's gifts, became obsessed with him, and began to devise ways to destroy him. Antonio was successful inasmuch as Mozart did die very young, but Antonio paid a hefty price for that success. Antonio's obsessive envy eventually drove him insane. Finally, only a shell of his former self, Antonio was left living amidst the grime and filth of an insane asylum, cursing God for denying him the kind of talent that was granted Mozart.

Envy is all about wanting what we don't have. There's one way to subdue this sin. It's through understanding the goodness of God. It's the virtue of contentment—a state of the heart, not a state of affairs. Whereas envy causes us to look horizontally—at what others have—contentment invites us to look vertically—at a good and gracious God. Envy creates discontent about the many things that we *don't* have; contentment brings satisfaction in the little that we *do* have. Envy focuses on excess; contentment rests in the simple pleasures and blessings of life.

Study Questions

1. What is the difference between jealousy and envy?

2. In what ways have you witnessed envy's destructive powers?

3. Why do you think envy is directed toward people close to us, not those who are distant from us?

4. Do you find that you often compare yourself with other people? How can you break this habit?

5.   In what ways has God been gracious to you and blessed you?

6.   How can you shift your focus from looking on others with envy to remembering the blessings of God?

4

CORRECTING ONE'S VISION

Mrs. Nguyen Thi An, a Vietnamese pastor's wife, was forced to live on a balcony outside an apartment with her children after police closed their church and threw her husband into prison. Without official papers, she was left homeless. Yet, her faith forged a sanctuary out of her surroundings. The government took her husband, her home, and her belongings, but they could not take her contentment. She wrote:

My Dear Friends,

. . . You know around here we are experiencing hardships, but we thank the Lord. He is comforting us and caring for us in every way. When we experience misfortune, adversity, distress and hardship, only then do we see the real blessing of the Lord poured down on us in such a way that we cannot contain it.

We have been obliged recently to leave our modest apartment and for over two months have been living on a balcony. The rain has been beating down and soaking us. Sometimes in the middle of the night we are forced to gather our blankets and run to seek refuge in a stairwell.

Do you know what I do then? I laugh and I praise the Lord, because we can still take shelter in the stairwell. I think of how many people are experiencing much worse hardships than I am. Then I remember the words of the Lord, "To the poor, O Lord, You are a refuge from the storm, a shadow from the heat" (cp. Isaiah 25:4), and I am greatly comforted. . . .

Our Father . . . is the One who according to the Scriptures does not break the bruised reed nor put out the flickering lamp. He is the One who looks after the orphan and the widow. He is the One who brings blessings and peace to numberless people.

I do not know what words to use in order to describe the love that the Lord has shown our family. I only can bow my knee and my heart and offer to the Lord words of deepest thanks and praise. Although we have lost our house and our possessions, we have not lost the Lord, and He is enough. With the Lord I have everything. The only thing I would fear losing is His blessing!

Could I ask you and our friends in the churches abroad to continue to pray for me that I will faithfully follow the Lord and serve Him regardless of what the circumstances may be?

As far as my husband is concerned, I was able to visit him this past summer. We had a 20-minute conversation that brought us great joy. . . .

I greet you with my love.

Mrs. Nguyen Thi An[1]

Despite her impoverished circumstances Mrs. Nguyen Thi An races far ahead of affluent Westerners in the achievement of contentment. Historian Arthur M. Schlesinger Jr. observes that our society is marked by "inextinguishable discontent."[2] Our quest is usually not for con-

---

1. Cited in Richard Swenson, M.D., *Margin* (Colorado Springs: NavPress, 1992), 189–90.
2. Ibid., 186.

tentment but for what is better and what is next. We want a better job with better pay and a better boss. We want better relationships and a better car and a better backhand in tennis or a longer drive in golf. And we have a propensity to live endlessly for the next thing—the next weekend, the next vacation, the next purchase, and the next experience. We are never satisfied, never content, and envious of those who have what we have not attained or accumulated.

What Mrs. Nguyen Thi An found is what we can find.

Contentment Defined

The author of Hebrews wrote, "Keep your lives free from the love of money and be content with what you have" (Heb. 13:5). Contentment lies not in what is mine but in whose I am. When I come into a relationship with God through his Son, Jesus Christ, I understand whose I am and what I have. Envy causes one to look horizontally—at what others have—so we are never satisfied. Contentment invites us to look vertically—at God. When we look in his direction, we know that he is enough.

John Stott wrote, "Contentment is the secret of inward peace. It remembers the stark truth that we brought nothing into the world and we can take nothing out of it. Life, in fact, is a pilgrimage from one moment of nakedness to another. So we should travel light and live simply. Our enemy is not possessions, but excess. Our battle cry is not 'Nothing!' but 'Enough!' We've got enough. Simplicity says, if we have food and clothing, we will be content with that."

Being content with less stuff and not envying those who have a lot is a process that will take more than a quick prayer, reading a book, or hearing a sermon.

Contentment Is Learned

The apostle Paul wrote, "I know what it is to be in need, and I know what it is to have plenty. I have learned the secret of being content in any and every situation, whether well fed or hungry, whether living in plenty or in want" (Phil. 4:12). Paul learned contentment in the circumstances of life, having more or having less. He learned this attitude in his relationship with Christ, who strengthened him. It is in that relationship that we, too, learn the lesson of contentment.

Contentment is learned. It isn't natural. We're not born with it. It is not a gift.

Our tendency is to look for things that will make us content—those things that are better or those events that are next—rather than putting forth the effort required to learn how to be content. The first time I took a group of students snow skiing, several of the older teenagers didn't want to "learn." They just wanted to ski like the rest of the people on the slope. Skiing isn't like that, and neither is becoming content. It takes a willingness and an effort to learn anything. We can't just wish things into existence. Contentment is no different. It, too, must be learned.

When several of the men who had been prisoners during the Vietnam War returned home after surviving the horrors of Hanoi, a number of those brave men said, "We learned after a few hours what it took to survive, and we just adapted to that." They didn't whine or complain because they had been captured. They learned contentment.

And so must we.

Contentment Is Internal

Contentment isn't denying one's feelings about wanting and desiring what one can't have; instead, it exhibits a freedom from being controlled by those feelings. Contentment isn't pretending that things are right when they are not; instead, it displays the peace that comes from knowing that God is bigger than any problems and that he works them all for our good. Contentment isn't a feeling of well-being contingent on keeping circumstances under control; instead, it promotes a joy in spite of circumstances, looking to God, who never varies. Contentment is of the heart. Contentment is not based on external circumstances but rather on an internal source.

Some people are like thermometers whereas others are like

thermostats. Some people merely register what is around them. If the situation is tight and pressurized, they register tension and irritability. If it's stormy, they register worry and fear. If it's calm, quiet, and comfortable, they register relaxation and peacefulness.

Other people, however, are like thermostats. They regulate the atmosphere. They have an inner source of satisfaction and power that never allows the situation to dictate them.

The majority of people in our society are like thermometers and suffers from pseudohappiness, a counterfeit high that evaporates quickly. They hope the next superficial satisfaction will last, but external happiness is like cotton candy—it's sweet for a moment and dissolves an instant later. A person who is happy because she is vacationing on Maui is a person who has only a few days to be happy. But a person who has learned to cultivate deep contentment will be a consistently joyful person wherever they are.

Most people thirst for what the apostle Paul had: enduring contentment, a deep, soul-satisfying contentment. That kind of contentment can come only from within. Contentment is always an inside job. It has everything to do with what is going on inside you, not what is going on outside. It has only one source. That source is found in a soul-satisfying relationship with our heavenly Father, who cares for us and promises to meet us where we are.

Contentment Is Surrender

Contentment is a matter of accepting from God's hand what he sends because we know that he is a good God and wants to give good gifts to his children. We accept, therefore, from God's hand that which he gives. All that is needful he will supply. He can redeem even pain and suffering that seemingly cannot be corrected.

Surrender is not dying as a person or being used and abused by those who are more powerful. Surrender is like taking the vacation of a lifetime and having someone come alongside you to take care of all of the details.

If we fail to surrender, we will forever be discontent. Our freedom will be suffocated. We will be in bondage to our desires. Our relationships will be poisoned with jealousy and competition. Potential blessings will be sacrificed. Discontentment has the potential to destroy our peace, rob us of joy, make us miserable, and tarnish our witness. We dishonor God if we proclaim a Savior who satisfies and then live discontentedly.

Contentment Is Hidden

The things that we expect to bring contentment surprisingly do not. We cannot depend upon contentment to fall into our laps from education, money, or status because contentment arises from a divine source that money and material possessions cannot purchase.

The secret of contentment is hidden from the casual observer. What is that secret?

Remember the Cross. The cornerstone of contentment is the Cross. Remember what Jesus has done for us on the Cross. Because of the Cross, we are freed from the chains of sin, including the sin of envy. Because of the Cross, our salvation is secure. Because of the Cross, our friendship with God is possible. Because of the Cross, our future in heaven is guaranteed. Isn't that enough? What else really matters? God has already taken care of the really big things!

Let go of the past. We cannot ever hope to gain contentment while holding on to past failures and mistakes either of others or of ourselves. There's a difference, however, between ignoring past wrongs and forgetting them. Forgetting means that we work through the process of forgiving others and allowing God's forgiveness to cover us. We need to let go of such statements as "I should have," "If only," and "If they hadn't." True forgiveness requires that we see the wrongs clearly, articulate them, release them to God, and then walk away from them. This process might take some time and require some assistance, but without it we will never have a contented heart.

Live one day at a time. Here we wait on God. We need to surrender our timetable and future to him. Envy comes from a wrong focus. If we focus on things and others, we will be discontent. But if we focus on God, living each day in the light of his glory, the things of this earth will pale in comparison.

Find sufficiency in Jesus Christ. The term *contentment* suggests "self-sufficiency." But in the context of the New Testament it means being at peace with Christ's sufficiency. When his powerful presence is consuming us, we can do all things. Christ has not given us unlimited strength, but we can experience contentment because we are continual recipients of supernatural strength. Our human determination might help us to endure adversity and pain, and our emotional toughness will help us get through job loss and financial hardships, but only Christ can generate a contented spirit within us amidst all that is happening around us.

Contrary to the attitude communicated by the sin of envy, those people who die with the most toys are not the ones who win. The winners are those who have loved their families well and know the joy of having that love returned. They are those who have known what it is to spend their lives for a purpose that is greater than themselves. They are those who have known their God and look forward to eternity with him.

Rudyard Kipling once told a class of graduating seniors not to care too much for the material, power, or fame. "Some day you will meet a man of such stature that he will care for none of these things . . . and then you will recognize how poor you are."[3] The real measure of wealth is how much we would be worth if we lost all of our stuff. Let's start measuring our value not by the things we have but by the things for which we would not take any amount of money. Then, and only then, will we correct the evil eye of envy.

In the final analysis, contentment lies not in what is ours but in whose we are. True contentment is impossible apart from the supernatural work of Christ in our lives.

---

3. Cited in Clyde E. Fant Jr. and William M. Pinson Jr., eds., *20 Centuries of Great Preaching* (Waco, Tex.: Word Books, 1971), 12:337.

Study Questions

1. Arthur M. Schlesinger, Jr., observes that our society is marked by "inextinguishable discontent." Make a list of the elements of discontent in your life.

2. If contentment is learned, then how has it been taught in your life?

3. Contrast the pretense of false contentment with the inner joy of true contentment.

4. Reflect on the statement, "Contentment lies not in *what* is ours but in *whose* we are."

5. What areas of your life have you surrendered to God? How has that affected your contentment?

6. We know intellectually that Christ is sufficient, but why don't we allow him to be sufficient in all areas of our lives? In what areas do you need the sufficiency of Christ to dwell?

The Sin of Anger

THE RAGING FIRE

It was the perfect vacation plan. My family and I would spend ten days on a Florida beach after visiting Disney World in Orlando. Being a frugal person, I arranged for our family to spend two nights at a motel free of charge—all we had to do was to attend a time-share presentation. No problem. We had attended one before with this same company, and it had been brief and painless. The meeting was at 9:00 A.M. We'd be out in fifteen minutes and on our way to see Mickey and Minnie before the gates opened at 10:00 A.M.

The next morning, we arrived in the lobby for the quick meeting only to discover at least twenty-five other people waiting for the brief presentation. *This is not looking good,* I thought, my blood pressure rising. Adding to my discomfort, we were informed that the sales presentation was at another resort. Being an eternal optimist, I commented, "This is good. We get to ride in a van. We might arrive at Disney a few minutes after it opens, but we will still have the entire day and night there. Anyway, breakfast is served at the other place." My wife and daughter met my justification with cold stares.

Thirty minutes later, we drove into the beautifully landscaped resort for the sales presentation. Ushered into a waiting room with one hundred other people, I grabbed a Danish and some orange juice before we were paired with a sales associate. I told her, "We are not interested. We want to hurry through the presentation so we can see Disney World."

"No problem," she said. "You know, all the locals go about 11:00 A.M. anyway to miss the crowds of tourists wanting to be there before the gates open." I looked at my wife. She didn't say anything, but I could read her face, and, believe me, it was not good.

As we walked to the individual presentation room, the sales person asked, "And what do you do for a living, Mr. Ezell?"

Now I want to make a confession. I am proud of the fact that I am a pastor. But sometimes I would rather people not know my occupation. When others know, their demeanor changes, as well as their expectations—at least my perception of their expectations—of me.

About half way through the presentation, I got "the look" from my wife, and I heard for the hundredth time my daughter ask, "Can we go, Daddy? You promised we would be at Disney World when it opened!" I said to the sales associate, "We are ready to go."

But she had a hook. "You don't want to lose your fifty dollar deposit, do you?"

Being a frugal person, I replied, "No!" But I could feel my face getting red.

"Well, you will have to tour the model condo."

"Okay," I said angrily, "but can we hurry?"

By this time, I was getting hotter and hotter. My plans had been thwarted. The sales person did not deliver on several things that she had promised. I was being made to feel guilty because I did not want, in the sales associate's words, "to experience luxury living for a week every year for the rest of my life." Hurriedly, we walked through the condo and returned to the main lobby where we stood in line to receive the fifty dollars. The sales person, in an attempt to make small talk, asked, "I hope you had an enjoyable experience."

By this time I was boiling. "No," I said, "I didn't have an enjoyable experience. I told you we weren't interested, yet you went through the whole presentation. Then you tried to make me feel guilty for not signing up today. You promised information throughout the presentation, yet you did not deliver. You lied to me. My family won't talk to me. I promised to have them at Disney World when it opened, and now we will be lucky to arrive by noon."

As I finished my remarks, we were at the window, where I would get back my fifty dollars. The sales associate said to the young lady behind the window, "He's not a happy camper."

The lady at the window said to me sarcastically, "Well, are we having a bad day?"

Honestly, I had to grit my teeth and hold back my temper—no, my rage. (After all, I was a pastor, and pastors aren't suppose to lose their cool, especially in public.) I was so angry that I wanted to reach through the window to strangle her.

At that moment, I could identify with Regina Barreca writing in the *Chicago Tribune Magazine*, ". . . anger is . . . an itch, an allergic reaction to some little piece of life's pollen blown your way."[1] Of all of the emotions, anger is probably the most common and most powerful. Hardly a day goes by without my experiencing some measure of anger—either my own or that of someone with whom I interact. My flight is delayed. The traffic is jammed. My daughter walks on the new carpet with mud on her shoes. A drunken driver kills three students at the local high school. I'm furious. My anger causes my face to turn red, my heart to race, and my eyes to water. I want to hit something or someone. The fire rages within. Anger is intensely personal. It is the quintessential individual signature emotion: I am what makes me mad.

Please understand, however, that anger is normal and healthy. I am not responsible for the event or person that brought on my anger; I am responsible for only how I respond to and use anger once it arises. The apostle Paul understood this fact when he wrote, "In your anger do not sin" (Eph. 4:26). Anger is not always sin. And not all anger is wrong. In the Old Testament, God became angry at the sin and wickedness of his people. In the New Testament, God's Son became indignant over the misuse of the temple. And humans are instructed to express their anger,

---

1. Regina Barreca, "The Fires Within," *Chicago Tribune Magazine*, 10 September 1995, 23.

but not to become full of wrath and hatred. But anger can cause sin. A difference exists between "an angry person" and "a person who is angry." An angry person is one who is controlled by anger—the fire is raging, leading to sin. A person who is angry, on the other hand, is someone who has allowed a bit of life's sparks from a certain event or person to ignite his anger—it's a fire but not a wildfire.

Igniting the Fire

"Anger," wrote Horace, "is a short madness."[2] My experience in Florida with the time-share presentation exemplifies the primary situations or feelings of my "short madness."

Fatigue. The previous day had been spent traveling to Florida. Traveling is for me, as it is for many people, a stressful event. I had not slept well in an unfamiliar bed the night before. I had to get up an hour earlier because we were in the Eastern time zone. I was tired, run down, and hungry. These kinds of situations and feelings always make me more susceptible to anger.

Embarrassment. I was embarrassed first by the sales associate because she was trying to make me feel guilty for not wanting to provide vacations for my family and accusing me of not wanting to live a good life. And then, to top it off, the young lady at the window made her sarcastic remark about having a bad day. When I am belittled or demoralized publicly, it often results in my getting angry.

Frustration. The most common cause of my anger is having my plans thwarted. When something upsets my plans, it ticks me off. Adding to my frustration in Florida, my thwarted plans also seriously affected my family.

Rejection. Because my plans were thwarted, I was feeling rejected by my family. They were hurt and I was hurt. And when I am hurt, anger most often rears its ugly head and begins to smolder.

Anger is an emotion that we all experience, but it is a secondary

---

2. John Bartlett and Justin Kaplan, eds., *Bartlett's Familiar Quotations,* 16th ed. (Boston: Little, Brown and Co., 1992), 97.

emotion that is caused by the primary problems of fatigue, embarrassment, frustration, or rejection. Understanding what starts the fire will help me control my anger.

Keeping the Fire Under Control

What should I do the next time my smokestack starts to blow? Good question. I need to learn to control my anger. Someone said, "Your temper is one of your most valuable possessions. Don't lose it."

Solomon wrote, "If you cannot control your anger, you are helpless as a city without walls, open to attack" (Prov. 25:28 GNB). "A fool gives full vent to his anger, but a wise man keeps himself under control" (29:11).

Aristotle was right, "Anybody can become angry—that is easy; but to be angry with the right person, and to the right degree, and at the right time, and for the right purpose, and in the right way—that is not within everybody's power and is not easy."[3]

If I can't control my anger, it will control me. So how do I keep the fires of my anger under control?

I can't bury my anger. When my wife and I were in London one spring, we discovered that some of the bombs dropped on England during World War II are still killing people. Sometimes they are discovered and sometimes blow up at construction sites, in fishing nets, or on beaches more than fifty years after the war. Undetected bombs become more dangerous with time because corrosion can expose the detonator.

What is true of bombs that are not dealt with is also true of people who have unresolved anger. Buried anger explodes when we least expect it. And when anger explodes, it does all sorts of damage. It severs relationships. It causes ulcers. It leads to murder. When anger is turned inward, it leads to depression. When it is turned outward, it leads to aggression. So I have to deal with my anger, not bury it.

---

3. Cited in Les Parrot, III, *High-Maintenance Relationships* (Wheaton, Ill.: Tyndale House, 1996), 130.

Anger is like a splinter in your finger. If you leave it there, it gets infected and hurts every time you use your finger. If you remove it, the sore heals and you feel better.

I have to be wary of chronically angry people. Solomon writes, "Do not make friends with a hot-tempered man, do not associate with one easily angered, or you may learn his ways and get yourself ensnared" (Prov. 22:24–25). Anger is highly contagious. I have discovered that it is dangerous for me to associate closely with people for whom anger has become a chronic way of life.

A story is told about two men who were hunting on a friend's ranch. When the two men reached the ranch, the driver told his buddy to wait in the truck while he checked with the owner of the ranch. The rancher gave them permission to hunt, but he asked for a favor. The rancher had a pet mule that was going blind, and he didn't have the heart to put him out of his misery. He asked that the hunters shoot the mule for him before they went hunting. When the driver came back to the pickup, he pretended to be angry. He scowled and slammed the door. His buddy asked him what was wrong.

"That no-good rancher told us we can't hunt. I'm so mad at that guy," the driver said, "I'm going out to his barn and shoot one of his mules!"

He drove like a maniac to the barn. His buddy protested, but the driver was adamant. "Just watch me!" he shouted. When they got to the barn, the driver jumped out of the truck with his rifle, ran inside, and shot the mule. As he was leaving, though, he heard two shots, and he ran back to the truck. He saw that his buddy had taken out his rifle, too. "What are you doing?" he yelled.

His buddy yelled back, face red with anger, "We'll show that son of a gun! I just killed two of his cows!"

If we are not careful, the anger of those with whom we associate will rub off on us. Their rage will become ours.

I have to take time to cool off. We should never speak in the heat of anger. We tend to say words that hurt or wound. Sometimes we say things that we never intended to say. We should give ourselves time to cool off because we want our anger to accomplish something positive. Eugene Peterson paraphrased Psalm 37:8 thus: "Bridle your anger, trash your wrath, cool your pipes—it only makes things worse" (*The Message*).

Often, when I am angry, my mouth runs faster than my mind. I engage my mouth before my mind is in gear. A sharp tongue only cuts one's throat. Someone knew what he was talking about when he said, "If you are angry, count to ten; if you are very angry, count to a hundred."

When I feel the fires of anger heating up, I ask myself, *Is this anger really worth what it's going to do to others and me emotionally? Will I make a fool of myself? Will I hurt someone I love? Will I lose a friend? Am I seeing this event from the other person's point of view?*

Many insignificant matters are not worth getting worked up about. We can win some battles and still lose the war. Perhaps one of the greatest cures for anger is delay.

I have to choose to forgive. Anger is a choice. I am reminded of that fact every time I am in an argument with my wife and the phone rings. If you are like me, you don't answer the phone with the same tone of voice that you are using in your fight. In a split second, I can go from screaming to my calm, pastoral voice as I say, "Hello." If anger is a choice, so is forgiveness. I can control my anger by choosing forgiveness over anger. The apostle Paul wrote, "Get rid of all bitterness, rage and anger, brawling and slander, along with every form of malice. Be kind and compassionate to one another, forgiving each other, just as in Christ God forgave you" (Eph. 4:31–32). Forgiveness is surrendering my right to hurt you back if you hurt me. It means that when I am the object of anger that I don't deserve, I can choose to forgive by not trying to strike back.

Forgiveness and anger cannot live together. I cannot be resentful and forgiving at the same time. If anger is fire, then forgiveness is water, the water that puts out the fire of anger.

I would like to be able to say that on that morning in Florida, after I cooled off, I went back to the sales associate and the lady at the window and asked their forgiveness, but I did not. But, hopefully, the next time something similar happens I will. In the meantime, I must learn how to lower the temperature of my anger.

Study Questions

1. List some of the "land mines" in your life.

2. What have been some of the consequences of your uncontrolled anger?

3. "Not all anger is sin." What does that statement mean to you?

4. Define forgiveness.

5. How does forgiveness quench the fires of anger?

Lowering the Temperature

Vera Czermak of Prague discovered that her husband was cheating on her. In her anger, she contemplated both murder and suicide, and chose the latter, leaping blindly out of her third-story window. She incurred only minor injuries, however, because she landed on her husband in the street below, killing him. The story concluded, "Sometimes, in this life, there is justice."

Yes, I suppose that sometimes there is justice. Unfortunately, many people don't know what justice is; therefore, they don't know it when they see it. The Old Testament prophet Micah declared, "What does the LORD require of you? To act justly and to love mercy and to walk humbly with your God" (Mic. 6:8). If we are to act justly, it stands to reason that we should know how to act. Another Old Testament prophet proclaimed, "Let justice roll on like a river, righteousness like a never-failing stream" (Amos 5:24). If we are to let justice roll on like a river, then we had better know how it rolls. The Pentateuch reminds us, "Follow justice and justice alone, so that you may live and possess the land the LORD your God is giving you" (Deut. 16:20). If we are to follow justice, then we had better know what to follow.

An understanding and practice of biblical justice enables us to lower the temperature of our emotions that would cause anger to flare up. Before we examine just what this justice is, allow me to dispel some misunderstandings about justice.

The Misconceptions of Justice

Justice is judgment. In current American jargon, the word *justice* very often connotes "judgment" or "punishment." We say that justice has been served, for example, when a criminal receives proper punishment for crimes committed. The biblical idea of justice is much broader and richer than the popular conception. Especially in the Old Testament, justice means fulfillment of the covenant. Although the punishment of lawbreakers is itself a fulfillment of the covenant, the prophets contend that justice is executed by positive and righteous action. Justice involves living in covenant relationship with God. Justice embraces the whole of the law, but the prophets agree with Jesus that loving God, loving one's neighbor, and loving oneself epitomizes the Law.

Justice is fairness. We want to equate justice with fairness because we have been taught from an early age that equal persons deserve equal treatment. Anyone who has watched small children argue over the division of a candy bar would agree that the notion of fairness—that everyone deserves equal treatment—seems to be present in humans from an early age.

Fairness is partial. It is subjective and based on arbitrary emotional consideration. It emphasizes personal rights while seeking to protect temporal values. It will always breed division and rebellion, and quite often it results in anger.

In trying to enforce traffic laws "fairly," a California policeman testified, "I have found that when I attempt to be 'fair,' I inevitably cite those who should have been warned, and warn those who should have been cited."

On the other hand, justice is impartial. It is objective and unemotional. It emphasizes personal responsibility while based on protecting eternal values. That is why the blindfold expresses the impartiality of justice on the statue of Justice that adorns courthouses across America.

Justice is mercy. I'm sure that you have heard the story about the lady who visited her photographer to sit for a portrait. She insisted to the photographer that he should "do her justice." The photographer was young. He did not know better. He replied, "Lady, you don't need justice; what you need is mercy."

Justice requires full payment for every violation. Mercy is withholding the punishment of our transgression. Justice is what we deserve. Mercy is what we need.

The Heart of Justice

Although justice includes an element of judgment and a component of fairness and a pinch of mercy, displaying and demonstrating justice moves beyond these ingredients. The virtue of justice involves being in right relationship with our fellow humans within the community.

In biblical times, justice involved a whole web of relationships that stemmed from Israel's covenant with God. Although the punishment of lawbreakers was itself a fulfillment of the covenant, and everyone was given his fair due, and, as always, mercy was called for, the prophets and the psalmists contended that justice was executed by caring and compassionate action toward everyone in the community. Moses said that the test case of whether a person or a community was just centered on how the marginalized people were treated; "For the LORD your God is God of gods and Lord of lords, the great God, mighty and awesome, who shows no partiality and accepts no bribes. He defends the cause of the fatherless and the widow, and loves the alien, giving him food and clothing. And you are to love those who are aliens, for you yourselves were aliens in Egypt" (Deut. 10:17–19).

The prophet Isaiah echoed those words: "Seek justice, encourage the oppressed. Defend the cause of the fatherless, plead the case of the widow" (Isa.1:17). The Israelites were to father the fatherless and feed the stranger, not because the orphan and the outsider deserved it, but because that was how God had acted toward Israel. For Israel, the practice of justice was an expression of love—God's love for them and their own love for others.

When we show justice, we mirror the loving God who has delivered us from sinful oppression. We act toward others as God has acted toward us. The evidence of justice, then, is when a community embraces those who are the most helpless. When we are compassionate toward others, then we view life from their perspective.

John, the apostle of love, gets to the heart of this matter. He writes, "If anyone has material possessions and sees his brother in need but has no pity on him, how can the love of God be in him? Dear children, let us not love with words or tongue but with actions and in truth" (1 John 3:17–18). Justice is not an abstract word about laws or rights. In the current world situation, perhaps another word for justice is love. If a Christian believer fails to help the hurting and care for the wounded, he or she is lacking the one essential ingredient of Christianity and justice—love.

The Soul of Justice

In fact, the soul of justice is summarized in what we call the Golden Rule: "In everything, do to others what you would have them do to you, for this sums up the Law and the Prophets" (Matt. 7:12). This statement has been called the Mount Everest of ethics, the uppermost peak of the greatest sermon in history. Jesus was saying that if we want the Cliff Notes of the Bible's entire teaching about justice, this absolutely outlandish and revolutionary statement is it. Furthermore, he was saying that if we want to defeat the demons of anger, we must practice and apply this irrefutable law. What's more, he wasn't saying that we should abide by this rule only when we feel like it, but that it should become a day-in, day-out lifestyle of compassion and caring.

Just imagine what the world would be like if everyone were to live by the Golden Rule. We wouldn't have to lock our doors at night. We wouldn't worry about our children playing at the park without us. Sales of "The Club" would plummet. No racism, no hate crimes, no slayings in Bosnia, and no starvation in Somalia would exist. Nations could spend their military budgets on feeding and clothing people and finding cures for AIDS and cancer. We would have no reason or cause for anger.

The world isn't like that, though. And the problem isn't that the Golden Rule is too esoteric or too complicated to understand. The problem is that we are primarily selfish people who are too preoccupied with our own well-being to help those who are hurting. Yet, as followers of Christ supernaturally empowered by the Holy Spirit, we can help change a little corner of our world if we put this rule into action and display the virtue of justice. Here's how.

See people through heaven's eyes. We have a tendency when we look at other people only to focus on the outside, which is soiled by sin. We see the rebellion and the failure, the dirt and the grime, and we miss the image of Almighty God. We are so valued and loved individually that God was willing to pay the infinite price of his Son's death to clean away our sin and restore us to himself.

In the song "In Heaven's Eyes," Phil McHugh pictured people as God sees them, and he found no worthless losers and no hopeless causes. When we see people from God's perspective, we suddenly have a new inspiration to treat them with the same dignity, respect, and honor that we desire for ourselves.

Crawl into someone's life. In whatever situation we are, we need to see the circumstance from the viewpoint of others. This merely means that we're more inclined to treat others as we'd like to be treated when we put ourselves in their shoes and see their predicament from their angle. The apostle Paul said, "Carry each other's burdens, and in this way you will fulfill the law of Christ" (Gal. 6:2). How can we carry another person's burden until we understand the burden as he or she sees it? When we crawl into someone else's life to view the world from their perspective, it will transform our whole attitude. Suddenly, we'll be more willing to help them, as we'd want to be helped.

Love from beyond ourselves. The Golden Rule must be fueled by love because our motivation is based primarily on what we can get in return. Once, someone asked Jesus what God's greatest law is, and he answered in two parts: "'Love the Lord your God with all your heart and will all your soul and with all your mind and with all your strength.' The second is this: 'Love your neighbor as yourself'" (Mark 12:30–31). Do you see why the order of those two laws is so critical?

When we open up our lives to God, receive his grace, and understand where we would be if it were not for him, he begins to shrink our self-centeredness and simultaneously enlarge our capacity to be more caring toward others. When it comes to the Golden Rule and justice, you do not start with your neighbor; you start with God. Loving God is what ultimately enables us to love others.

Making a choice to make a difference. Plain and simple, doing for others what you want them to do for you is an act of the will. We must decide consciously to pursue and demonstrate justice. Otherwise, our busyness will prevent us from pausing long enough to consider others. Or sometimes we get intimidated into inaction, because we see the mountain of needs in the world. It's so easy to forget this fundamental truth: no expression of compassion to another human being is a wasted effort.

This truth struck me afresh when I was reading the words of a new volunteer who had gone to serve with Mother Teresa among the poorest of the poor in Calcutta. On their tour of a children's home, Mother Teresa spotted an infant who had been rescued from the streets but who was beyond medical help. The child was surely going to die that day.

So Mother Teresa picked up the baby and handed her to the new volunteer, offering these simple instructions: "Don't let this child die without being loved."

Later, the volunteer said, "I held her in my arms and I loved her until she died at six o'clock in the evening. I spent the hours humming Brahms' Lullaby, and do you know—*I could feel that baby, as tiny and as weak as she was, pressing herself against me.*"[1] Even a dying infant responds to a simple act of human kindness.

We don't have to take it upon ourselves to change the world. Let's

---

1. Kathryn Spink, *The Miracle of Love* (San Francisco: Harper and Row, 1981), 124–25, emphasis added.

face it. We can't do that anyway. But just in the course of everyday life—from common courtesies to going out of our way to assist those in need—doing to others what we would want them to do to us will make a difference in both their lives and our own. And what is more, we will demonstrate the virtue of justice, thereby throwing water on the fires of anger.

Study Questions

1. How does a biblical understanding of justice prevent anger from flaring into sin?

2. How does Jesus sum up justice?

3. Reflect on how God chose to look at you with love rather than anger.

4. How will looking at people from God's perspective help control the fires of anger?

5. What is the significance of loving God first and then people, as instructed in the first and second great commandments?

6. What positive actions can you take toward those who have wronged you?

THE SIN OF SLOTH

LIVING ON THE BENCH

In Elie Wiesel's autobiographical novel *The Town Beyond the Wall,* he tells the story of Michael. Michael, a young Jew who survived the Holocaust, traveled at great personal risk behind the Iron Curtain to his Hungarian hometown. Although his memory burned with images of the soldiers and police who had brutalized him and those whom he loved, Michael returned not for revenge, but to satisfy his curiosity.

"This, this was the thing I had wanted to understand ever since the war. Nothing else. How a human being can remain indifferent."[1]

In a strange way he understood the brutality of the executioners and the prison guards. What he did not understand was the man whom Wiesel called a spectator who lived across from the synagogue, the man who peered through his window day after day as thousands of Jews were herded into the death trains. His face "was gazing out, reflecting no pity, no pleasure, no shock, not even anger or interest. Impassive, cold, impersonal. The face was indifferent to the spectacle."[2]

There is a bond, Michael thought, between the brutal executioner and the victim, even though the bond is negative. ". . . they belong to

---

1. Elie Wiesel, *The Town Beyond the Wall* (New York: Atheneum, 1964), 149.
2. Ibid., 150.

the same universe; . . . But this is not true of that Other. The spectator is entirely beyond us. He sees without being seen. He is there but unnoticed."[3]

Wiesel concludes, "To be indifferent—for whatever reason—is to deny not only the validity of existence, but also its beauty. Betray, and you are a man; torture your neighbor, you're still a man. Evil is human, weakness is human; indifference is not."[4]

Indifference is a deadly sin. It is to be forever a spectator on the sidelines of life. *Sloth* is the old term that contains two components: *acedia,* which means a lack of caring, an aimless indifference to one's responsibilities to God and to man, and *tristitia,* meaning sadness and sorrow leading to a final stage of despair, hence, its deadly nature.

Interestingly, pride and sloth represent opposite sins, both of which are deadly. Pride is an attempt to be more than human, to be God; sloth, on the other hand, is to be less than human, merely a spectator, indifferent to human life and the human race. In the Garden of Eden, pride sought God's throne; sloth ran from the Garden. Pride takes God's role; sloth escapes human responsibility.

The devil's strategy with pride is to attack us not at our weakness but at our strength. With sloth, however, he pulls a reverse and attacks us at our weakness. Sloth makes us like a spectator, preventing us from getting in the game in support of a good cause. It won't allow us to leave our comfortable seat to run risks; the demands and the costs are too great. We are bundled in a self-protective coat, fearful of any expression of emotion or show of vulnerability.

The church fathers catalogued indifference as one of the seven deadly sins. In our modern world, however, as we've done with so many of our other sins, we have given it a new name, perhaps to ease our conscience or to avoid responsibility. We might call it laziness, apathy, tolerance, or despair. Whatever we call it, it is the sin that believes in nothing, cares for nothing, seeks to know nothing, interferes with nothing, enjoys nothing, loves nothing, hates nothing, finds pur-

---

3. Ibid., 151.
4. Ibid., 177.

pose in nothing, and lives for nothing, and it remains alive only because it would die for nothing. It forever remains on the sidelines, unmoved, uncaring, uninvolved.

The Arenas of Indifference

One does not have to look far or hard to find spectators. People watch from the sidelines in a multitude of arenas. Indifference is commonplace in our world. Just look around.

Relationships. Indifference prevents us from loving people. Think about it: indifference prevents us from putting the necessary energy into building and maintaining healthy relationships. It prevents us from disciplining our children; we choose instead the easy path of least resistance. It prevents us from getting involved with a neighbor who is hurting. It prevents us from contributing to a needy family or offering assistance to a new neighbor.

Purpose. Indifference poisons the will to live. Many people have died long before they were buried. The deadly disease of indifference sucks the life from an individual. They are here but not present. For all practical purposes, they are dead.

How can we tell? Easily. When the suffering of another causes us no pain, we're dead. When our blood does not run hot in the face of blatant injustice, we're dead. When we evade the truth that hurts and accept an easy life, we're dead. When we are not willing to put forth the energy necessary to save a dying relationship, we're dead.

People who have given up their will to live are numb; they are paralyzed. They have given up interest in pursing a meaningful life. They are like a rudderless raft on an open sea. They float aimlessly, taken wherever the current chooses. Remember, when we go with the flow, we always flow down.

Responsibility. Indifference promotes apathy toward responsibility. An old story tells of a fellow who said to a man at the bus stop, "The biggest problem in our country today is ignorance and apathy." To which the other fellow replied, "Well, I don't know and I don't care."

That is the attitude of indifferent spectators. They fail to take the steps necessary to find out what is going on in their world. They are too lazy to read, to think for themselves, or to enter into challenging dialogue. Instead, they take opinions from the newspaper columnists, television newscasters, and their favorite talk show hosts. They are ignorant, often masquerading as a collection of prejudices. Prejudice is a great labor-saving device; it enables a person to promote opinions without taking the trouble to get the facts.

In the end, indifferent people do nothing. They utter such pious-sounding phrases as, "Mind your own business," "Don't get involved," and "Live and let live." They become like the group of people who watched—as mere spectators—a woman being beaten to death by a gang of thugs and did nothing.

Spirituality. Indifference affects our spiritual direction. The spiritual moorings in life become foggy, and a spiritual vacuum ensues, manifesting itself in apathy toward spiritual things. Believers lose their joy in serving God and their zeal in worshiping God. They feel like spiritual weaklings, unable to live up to their expectations of the Christian life. They are saddened because they neglect their religious obligations, such as praying, attending church, confessing sin, reading the Bible, giving to the needy, and witnessing to the lost. They become spiritually dry and distant, possessing an unwillingness to seek and do the will of God.

I once had lunch with a friend who was similar to me in age and convictions about the Christian faith. My friend knew his Bible; he had been faithful in church leadership. His faith had once been a priority. As we talked, I could tell that my friend bordered on boredom as he talked about his spiritual struggles.

I asked, "Where are you these days with God?"

"Where am I with God?" he repeated the question as he looked away from me.

At least a thirty-second pause followed before he finally responded, "Do you really want to know?"

"Yeah, I'm your friend, and I'm interested," I responded.

"I'm not anywhere," he said, "and I haven't been anywhere for a long time. When it comes to my Christian life, I'm going through the motions. To be honest, I'm a spectator. I know I should be involved, be committed, give my part. But inside I'm as dry as a bone."

Spiritual indifference occurs when the spiritual quest becomes too demanding and nothing we do seems to make a difference. We become consumers rather than contributors, spectators rather than participants. We are like a car that is bright and shiny, but the gas tank is empty. We have action without heart, oratory without power, and doctrine without love.

Now one might say that in our society we don't have a problem with such indifference; perhaps in another time but not now. We are a society that is loud and bold and brash when it comes to our rights. We are not lazy or indifferent, are we?

Let's see if that statement is true. Let's account for each of those areas.

If indifference is not a problem in our relationships, then why do we have so many broken relationships? Why do so many divorces occur? Why are so many children and spouses being abused? Why are so many friendships thrown unsalvaged on the rocks?

If indifference is not a problem in our purpose for living, then why do we have a plethora of self-help books and motivational seminars? Why are we busy but not achieving anything? Why do we enjoy the good life, but not a meaningful life?

If indifference is not a problem in regard to our responsibility, then why do so few people go to the polls to vote? Why do we see an uncaring attitude toward injustice, abortion, or national debt or toward helping the lonely, the abused, and the poverty stricken?

If indifference is not a problem on the spiritual side of life, then why are we seeking desperately for meaning and for life to make sense? Why does it seem that our spiritual life is as dry as the Sahara? Why do we care so little about God? Why have Christians forgone Jesus' Great Commission and developed a universalist attitude toward people, believing—no, hoping—that in the end God will save everyone?

If you find yourself on the bench of life and wanting to get in the game, there is hope. There is a way for you to get off the bench.

Study Questions

1. What are some modern words we use to describe sloth? How is sloth a sin?

2. In what ways are you afraid to leave your comfort zones, to run a risk, to engage in a cause?

3. What relationships are in most need of your renewed attention?

4. What steps do you need to take to define your purpose for living?

5. What are the dangers of spiritual sloth?

6. What steps will you take to revitalize your spiritual life?

GETTING IN THE GAME

In the first few months of 1940, with the fate of France uncertain because of the impending threat of Nazi Germany, Britain withdrew its troops from mainland Europe. It was one of the most massive retreats in military history. Beginning on May 26, more than 330,000 Allied troops made the dangerous withdrawal across the English Channel on thousands of small, privately owned boats.

In the aftermath of this seemingly miraculous deliverance, England was in a mood of euphoria. The retreat had been pulled off successfully, and the British people celebrated as if they had won the war. But such an exodus was misleading. Victory had not been secured. Defeat had only been avoided—temporarily.

In an attempt to temper such ill-founded confidence, Prime Minister Winston Churchill stood behind the podium in the House of Commons on June 4 and sounded a sober note of reality. No victory could be claimed. "Wars are not won by evacuations!" he admonished.

Many historians considered it to be one of the greatest speeches ever delivered. It was a message worth a thousand guns, many people said. Typically stoic British House members cried. So did the manly Churchill.

The prime minister concluded his message by calling upon all

Englishmen to defend their island courageously to the death. As Churchill ended his now-famous address, he sought deliberately to infuse a defiant spirit into his fellow countrymen:

> We shall not flag or fail. We shall go on to the end. We shall fight in France, we shall fight on the seas and oceans, we shall fight with growing confidence and growing strength in the air, we shall defend our island, whatever the cost may be, we shall fight on the beaches, we shall fight on the landing grounds, we shall fight in the fields and in the streets, we shall fight in the hills; we shall never surrender.[1]

To win wars requires steel-willed resolve; a strong, inner fortitude; a deep dedication; and a sense of purpose. "Wars are not won by evacuations!"

Exactly two weeks after Churchill's stirring speech, on June 18, England braced itself for the inevitable Battle of Britain—Hitler's invasion by air. With the English people prepared to fight for their national survival, Churchill again addressed Parliament. His words called for iron-clad courage.

> Upon this battle depends the survival of Christian civilization. The whole fury and might of the enemy must very soon be turned on us. . . . Let us, therefore, brace ourselves to our duties, and so bear ourselves that if the British Empire and its Commonwealth last for a thousand years, men will still say, "This was their finest hour."[2]

That's how wars are won and societies are changed. Victory belongs not to the fainthearted nor to the weak willed, nor to the uncommitted. Not if the enemy is great and his resolution strong. Only by facing the adversary head on with undaunted valor can the battle

---

1. John Bartlett and Justin Kaplan, eds., *Bartlett's Familiar Quotations,* 16th ed. (Boston: Little, Brown and Co., 1992), 620.
2. Ibid.

be won. Victory necessitates that we fight on with undying, inflexible resolve and courage.

The Virtue of Courage

A woman and her husband interrupted their vacation to go to a dentist. "I want a tooth pulled, and I don't want Novocain because I'm in a big hurry," the woman said. "Just extract the tooth as quickly as possible, and we'll be on our way."

The dentist was quite impressed. "You're certainly a courageous woman," he said. "Which tooth is it?"

The woman turned to her husband and said, "Show him your tooth, dear."

Courage is something that we admire in others, isn't it? We write about it, acknowledge it, and applaud it. But courage is a virtue, not by choice but of necessity, found in people who defeat the sin of indifference.

Courage enabled a young sheep-herding teenager named David to go toe to toe with the giant Goliath. Courage empowered the prophet Elijah to stand against the prophets of Baal on Mount Carmel. Courage infused the three Hebrew boys—Shadrach, Meshach, and Abednego—empowering them to refuse to bow to the golden statue of Nebuchadnezzar. Courage enabled Daniel to stand for his religious convictions even when doing so meant being eaten alive by lions. Courage prompted a handful of uneducated disciples to proclaim boldly the message of Jesus Christ even in the face of persecution and possible death. Courage equipped Stephen to face the stones and rocks of hatred. In each of these instances, these people displayed courage. They refused to sit by idly. They refused to be spectators. They got off the bench and got into the game.

The necessity for courage is inherent in the Christian faith because the world is instinctively its enemy. Granted, varying degrees and forms of opposition exist. Sometimes it is violent and brutal; fires and swords have taken the lives of many professing believers. At other times, it is subtle and scornful; satire and comedy have also been weapons of choice in some societies. Let's face it, the spirit of this world is hostile to the Spirit of Christ. And the courage required to stand against the enemy sometimes might be greater when the opposition is subtle and soft-spoken than when it is violent and boisterous.

The apostle Paul wrote the following message to the church at Corinth: "Be on your guard; stand firm in the faith; be men of courage; be strong" (1 Cor. 16:13). That message to the first-century church is the same message that is given to the church of the twenty-first century. How do we stand firm and be people of courage so that we can move past indifference? What do we need to do to get off the bench and into the game?

Face Our Fears

Fear is debilitating. Fear grinds the gears of our lives to a halt. Fear destroys dreams and sabotages plans. Fear prevents us from starting our trek or standing our ground. Fear paralyzes us, making us unable to act. Fear is the biggest cause of inactivity.

And if you are afraid, rejoice, for you are in good company. Everyone gets afraid. Fear is a common emotion. Heroes are fearful. The brave are fearful. The confident are fearful. Courage is not the absence of fear but the ability to walk on in spite of it. Truthfully, courage knows what to fear. Fear is commonplace. Just because one is courageous does not mean that he is operating without fear.

If we are to win the fights, right the wrongs, and gain the victories over our enemies, we have to attack our fears first. The only way to defeat our fears is to walk toward the thing we fear. When we are bold, mighty forces will come to our aid. Boldness means making a deliberate decision to walk on in spite of our fears, knowing that mighty forces—both physical and mental—will assist us in our venture. For example, although a hurled pebble's centrifugal force killed Goliath, courage enabled David to face the Philistine giant in the first place. Likewise, similar forces came to the aid of Elijah, Daniel, Stephen, and all of the other heroes whom we named earlier.

A loving God spoke to a timid and fearful general who was about to lead his army in the most extensive battle of his life. God said to

Joshua, "Yes, be bold and strong! Banish fear and doubt! For remember, the Lord your God is with you wherever you go" (Josh. 1:9 TLB). Following Moses' death, God called upon Joshua to lead the people of Israel into the Promised Land. Undoubtedly, Joshua felt weak and afraid as he contemplated his monumental task. God gave him a pep talk. Four times God encouraged Joshua to be strong and courageous. Why? Joshua was no different from you or me. He was afraid. He had been in the land as a spy forty years earlier. He remembered the powerful people who inhabited the land and the well-protected cities. The task before him would not be a cake walk. He learned that it is much easier to face one's fears knowing that God is present and that all of the forces of heaven stand ready to assist.

Take a Stand

The apostle Paul spoke of courage when he wrote to the church at Thessalonica, "Yet God gave us the courage to boldly repeat the same message to you, even though we were surrounded by enemies" (1 Thess. 2:2 LB). Courage can be defined as the ability to do what is right even when we don't have to. Embedded in courage is conviction—the issues of the heart by which one will live and for which one will die. Convictions are the mainsprings of action, the driving powers of being, the embodiment of one's life. Martin Luther King Jr. often told his children, "If a man hasn't discovered something that he will die for, he isn't fit to live."[3] When we show our courage, we live out our convictions as we say no to the things that are wrong and yes to the things that are right.

The opposite of courage is not cowardice but conformity. The temptation to conform often is stated as "Be one of the boys," "Go along with the crowd," or "Come on, everyone is doing it." In some situations, we can't always walk away; that's when we are forced to take a stand. At such pivotal moments, surrounded by enemies, we show the crowd who we are and whom we serve.

---

3. Ibid., 760.

Martin Luther, the reformer, stood at the Wittenburg Chapel, nailing to the door his Ninety-five Theses that exposed the heresy and hypocrisy of the teaching that people had to pay for their sins to be forgiven. At the Diet of Worms on April 18, 1521, he stated, "Here I stand; I can do no other. God help me. Amen."[4]

Sometimes, we are forced to say the same thing in different ways: "Here I stand. I can do no other."

At a national sales convention, a heralded entertainer delivered his comedy routine. His presentation was punctuated with many curse words, lewd comments, and the taking of God's name in vain. Finally, a businessman in the audience could no longer remain silent. He rose from his seat, stood on his chair, and shouted to the performer, "Please leave God out of it!" The comedian cleaned up his performance. Afterward, more people lined up to shake the businessman's hand than that of the performer.

At a high school in my community, several students chosen for roles in the fall drama quit. They had been given only excerpts from the play for the audition. Once they were selected and given the entire script, they discovered that the play contained off-color language and innuendoes, and, in their opinion, was inappropriate for a high school play. As a result, these students chose not to participate. I admire their conviction and their courage to stand for their values.

Whatever your conviction, stand firm on it. The writer of Proverbs was right: "The wicked man flees though no one pursues, but the righteous are as bold as a lion" (Prov. 28:1). Be bold. Stand firm.

Act Bravely

At the heart of courage is action—getting in the game. To slay the dragon of inactivity and indifference, we have to move from the safe seats in the stands onto the playing field of action. As the apostle Paul reminded Timothy, "For God did not give us a spirit of timidity, but a spirit of power, of love and of self-discipline" (2 Tim. 1:7). Why? So we will act.

---

4. Ibid., 138.

A devout Christian who was a seamstress and a member of the Dexter Avenue Baptist Church in Montgomery, Alabama, believed that Jesus had something to teach a segregated world about love, justice, and community. One morning in December 1955, a bus driver told her that she must vacate her seat and move to the back of the bus because she was an African-American and a white person needed the seat. In one of the most courageous choices of the twentieth century, she did not move—and she started a revolution. The next Monday night, ten thousand people gathered at her church to pray and to ask God, "What do we do next?" Because of that choice, a revolution started that was not easy; it had a high cost. Many people were beaten, many people were imprisoned, and some people even died. But that revolution changed the conscience of a nation—all because a mild-mannered, soft-spoken, Christ-following seamstress dared to act.

Action is a rarity anymore. We are content to let the other person do it. We are apathetic about situations, causes, and problems. Or we feel overwhelmed by what we have to do. We have been sucked into the attitude that says that my vote, my effort, or my voice won't matter, so why bother. What if Jesus had displayed a similar attitude? Where would we be?

The movie *Chariots of Fire* was a story about two runners who were determined to win. Harold Abrahams was a Jewish student, and Eric Liddell was a Scot. Both men won gold medals at the 1924 Paris Olympics. One scene in the movie depicts Abrahams as being incredibly discouraged and wanting to quit after he lost a race to Liddell. He blurted to his friend, "I run to win. If I can't win, I won't run," to which his friend replied angrily, "If you don't run, you can't win!" Abrahams ran again—and won.

Inactivity never accomplished anything.

People who act become our heroes. They muster courage and inspire us to rise beyond our own inactivity and indifference.

Get into the Game

"Go to the ant, you sluggard; consider its ways and be wise!" (Prov. 6:6). No one has to tell an ant what to do; it just does it. They are creatures on the move.

Perhaps you've heard the story about the two ants on the golf course. A ball had landed close to them. The hacker started swinging his club and missed the ball. He did it once, then twice. One ant started scurrying toward the ball. The other asked where he was going. He said, "Follow me. If we don't get on the ball, we are going to die."

Getting into the game is doing what needs to be done. "The sluggard craves and gets nothing, but the desires of the diligent are fully satisfied" (Prov. 13:4). God put us on this earth to act. We must act courageously and diligently.

When it comes to relationships, the courageous take the time to develop the relationships. They invest the necessary energy. With their spouses, they make time for each other. With their children, they discipline rather than give in. With friends, they overlook petty faults because they care. With all relationships, they go the extra mile.

When it comes to purpose, the courageous find a reason for living. They discover how God has gifted them. They seek ways to help others. They give of themselves to a cause or an institution. They look beyond themselves. They agree with Edward Everett Hale, "I am only one, but still I am one. I cannot do everything, but still I can do something. Because I cannot do everything, let me not refuse to do the something that I can do."[5]

When it comes to responsibility, the courageous refuse to look the other way. They do their part and their fair share. They join an advocacy group. They share in the ministry of the church. They seek ways by which they can help in the community.

When it comes to spiritual direction, the courageous engage in the necessary disciplines to keep their bearings. They practice faithfully

---

5. *The Doubleday Christian Quotation Collection,* comp. Hannah Ward and Jennifer Wild (New York: Doubleday, 1998) 175.

prayer, fellowship, giving, service, church attendance, and reading and studying of Scripture. These spiritual disciplines keep the wells of refreshment and renewal full of fresh water, leaving their souls with no possibility of drying or parching.

The courageous live by three life-changing words: *DO IT NOW!* They refuse to delay or to procrastinate. They don't evacuate. They see what needs to be done and do it—now. They choose not to stand on the sidelines and merely watch. They get into the game.

Study Questions

1. Describe the most courageous act that you have ever witnessed.

2. In what ways does living as a Christian in a non-Christian world require courage?

3. What are your greatest fears that prevent you from standing for what is right?

4. What actions can you take to walk on in spite of your fears?

5. Of the four arenas of indifference—relationships, purpose for living, responsibility, and spiritual life—which causes you the most struggle? Why?

6. What action steps could you take to get off the bench of life and into the game?

THE SIN OF GREED

THE GRIP OF
CONSUMPTION

A prosperous, young investment banker was driving a new BMW sedan on a mountain road during a snowstorm. As he veered around one sharp turn, he lost control and began sliding off the road toward a deep precipice. At the last moment, he unbuckled his seat belt, flung open his door, and leaped from the car, which then tumbled down the ravine and burst into a ball of flames.

Although he had escaped with his life, the man suffered a ghastly injury. Somehow his arm had been caught near the hinge of the door as he jumped and had been severed at the shoulder.

A trucker saw the accident in his rearview mirror. He pulled his rig to a halt and ran to see if he could help. He found the banker standing at the roadside, looking down at the BMW burning in the ravine below.

"My BMW! My new BMW!" the banker moaned, oblivious to his injury.

The trucker pointed at the banker's shoulder and said, "You've got bigger problems than that car. We've got to find your arm. Maybe the surgeons can sew it back on!"

The banker looked where his arm had been, paused a moment, and groaned, "Oh no! My Rolex! My new Rolex!"

Although this story is fictional, the truth is relevant to our society today. We are a people obsessed with stuff. We have a need to own, to possess.

The Bible has a word for it—greed. Our culture is less inclined to see greed as a major source of human troubles—unless, I suppose, your arm is cut off. Rather, it sees greed as what makes the world go 'round. In a capitalistic society, it's not a vice but a virtue. It's a lifestyle that no one considers a sin anymore.

Perhaps you recall a few years ago when Ivan Boesky went to prison and paid a fine of $100 million for insider trading. Earlier in his career, he was the darling of Wall Street. During that time, he declared at the graduation ceremony of the School of Business Administration of the University of California, Berkeley, "Greed is all right, by the way. I want you to know that. I think greed is healthy. You can be greedy and still feel good about yourself."[1] As *Newsweek* commented later, "The strangest thing, when we come to look back, will be not just that Ivan Boesky could say that at a business school graduation but that it was greeted with laughter and applause."[2]

But greed is no laughing matter, and it definitely is not a virtue. Paul wrote, "The love of money is a root of all kinds of evil" (1 Tim. 6:10). Jesus warned, "Watch out! Be on your guard against all kinds of greed" (Luke 12:15). God takes greed and its effect on people very seriously. And so should we.

An Unsatisfied Desire

Practically speaking, greed is an inordinate desire for more, an excessive, unsatisfied hunger to possess. Greed is forever discontented. It thirsts for more and more of the things that we think we need to be truly satisfied. As when one drinks seawater, the more we drink of the

---

1. "True Greed," *Newsweek*, 1 December 1986, 48.
2. Ibid.

things that we think we need to be satisfied, the thirstier we become for more.

As a case in point, all that one particular man ever really wanted in life was more. He wanted more money, so he parlayed inherited wealth into a billion-dollar pile of assets. He wanted more fame, so he broke into the Hollywood scene and soon became a filmmaker and star. He wanted more sensual pleasures, so he paid handsome sums to indulge his every sexual urge. He wanted more thrills, so he designed, built, and piloted the fastest aircraft in the world. He wanted more power, so he secretly dealt political favors so skillfully that two U.S. presidents became his pawns. All he ever wanted was more. He was absolutely convinced that more would bring him true satisfaction. Unfortunately, history shows otherwise.

Although that man was one of the richest men in the world, he lived a sunless, joyless, half-lunatic life. When he died, his scraggly beard hung down to his waist, and his hair reached to the middle of his back. His fingernails were two inches long, and his toenails hadn't been trimmed for so long that they resembled corkscrews. His skin was emaciated and colorless. His teeth were rotting and black. His arms revealed innumerable needle marks from his drug addiction.

Howard Hughes died believing the myth that having more will make one happy. He died a billionaire junkie, insane by all reasonable standards.

In the never-enough world, the message that having more will make one happy is preached as though it were the gospel truth. Nearly every time I open a magazine, turn on the television, or talk to a neighbor, I am bombarded with the message that having more will provide the answers to life's basic questions and satisfy the longing of my soul.

I remember my first paycheck. I thought, *Who could ever want more money?* The answer came quickly enough: *me.*

I remember my first apartment. I thought, *Who could ever want more space to live?* The answer came just as quickly: *me.*

When I had my first book published, I thought, *Who would ever want another book published? Me.* It seems that no matter how much I have, I still want more.

The problem with greed is that rather than leading us to a higher level of living, it leads us to an impoverished level of living. It becomes like a cancer, eating away at our very life. This is what makes greed so deadly.

The Misconceptions of Greed

Why do we always want more? What motivates us to live beyond our means? Many misunderstandings abound concerning greed.

Having more things will make me happy. Fill in the blank in the following sentence: If only I had _____, I'd be happy. We are bombarded constantly by commercials and movies that communicate one basic message: you can buy happiness. No society has more stuff than our society. But are we happy? The Scripture says, "He who loves money shall never have enough. The foolishness of thinking that wealth brings happiness! The more you have, the more you spend" (Eccl. 5:10–11 TLB).

Is it true that having more will make me happy?

Most wealthy people will be the first to inform us that their millions have not brought them happiness. Billionaire Ross Perot puts the wealthy in perspective, "Guys, just remember, if you get real lucky, if you make a lot of money, if you go out and buy a lot of stuff—it's gonna break. You got your biggest, fanciest mansion in the world. It has air conditioning. It's got a pool. Just think of all the pumps that are going to go out. Or go to a yacht basin any place in the world. Nobody is smiling, and I'll tell you why. Something broke that morning. The generator's out; the microwave oven doesn't work. . . . Things just don't mean happiness."[3]

The reality of greed is that it often produces families who are unable to get off the treadmill because they are deeply in debt. Parents have no time for each other or their children. Often, we have nicer things than our parents had when they were our age but little time to enjoy them. Men and women know how to dress for success but are

---

3. Cited in Craig Brian Larsen, ed., *Illustrations for Preaching and Teaching* (Grand Rapids: Baker, 1993), 151.

full of doubts and questions on the inside. Those who have chased for more things and more money and caught it have run the rainbow out to its end and have found it an unexpectedly empty journey. "To Americans usually tragedy is wanting something very badly and not getting it," observed Henry Kissinger. "Many people have had to learn in their private lives . . . that perhaps the worst form of tragedy is wanting something badly, getting it, and finding it empty."[4]

The idea that having more will make me happy is a lie. The acquisition and accumulation of more is a cruel hoax that might provide a momentary surge in emotions, but it never lasts. Having more is never enough. It will never satisfy. It will not bring lasting happiness.

Having more things will make me more important. In other words, I am what I own. My valuables determine my value. Have you noticed that we buy things that we don't need with money we don't have to impress people we don't like. Jesus warned against this kind of behavior. He said, "Be on your guard against all kinds of greed; a man's life does not consist in the abundance of his possessions" (Luke 12:15). Jesus was saying not to confuse your net worth with your self-worth. Value is not based on valuables.

Having more things will make me more secure. I heard of a survey conducted among top executives who made incomes in the upper six figures. They were asked, "Do you feel you make enough money to be secure?" And the vast majority answered, "No." When the stock market falls, it only intensifies the insecurity of money and things. Talk of restructuring at work causes us to get nervous. When the economy goes south, so do our feelings of safety. Solomon was right when he wrote, "Whoever trusts in his riches will fall" (Prov. 11:28).

The Blunders of Greed

Jesus addressed the issue of money and material possessions on many occasions. In doing so, he had a unique way of getting to the heart of the matter. In the parable of the rich fool, found in Luke 12:13–21, Jesus

---

4. Cited in Richard A. Swenson, *Margin* (Colorado Springs: NavPress, 1992), 196.

uncovered three major mistakes often made by those who value life by their valuables, those who are caught in the grip of consumption.

First, let's understand that the rich farmer in Jesus' story was not condemned because he was successful and prosperous. There wasn't a word here or anywhere in Scripture against well-earned or well-deserved success or financial prosperity. This man was not denounced because he was lazy or dishonest. On the contrary, he apparently proved to be very diligent and careful as an agribusinessman. He planted and harvested. He seemed to have done everything correctly. So what he saw as he looked outside his window was a bumper crop. It must have been beautiful to behold. Nothing was wrong with having a bumper crop—or with any of the things that brought him prosperity. So what *was* wrong?

He made three glaring mistakes. And what was true of the farmer is also true for those of us who are caught in the grip of greed.

He mistook time for eternity. In response to the farmer's self-talk, "You have plenty of good things laid up for many years" (Luke 12:19), God said, "This very night your life will be demanded from you" (v. 20). The man never saw beyond this world. It never entered his mind that he might not live for many years to come; he talked to his soul as though he were immortal. He was so preoccupied with the temporal that he didn't bother to think about the eternal.

Here's a parallel story. A genie granted a businessman one wish. He told the genie that he wanted to see the stock market report for a year from that date so he could know ahead of time where to invest and make a killing.

The genie showed the businessman the stock market report for a year in the future. At first, he was excited, but then he froze in fear. On the other side of the page were the obituaries, and his picture was printed there.

It is a fictitious story, but you get the point. People who are caught in the grip of greed tend to prepare for time but not for eternity. But one is not ready to live tomorrow until he is ready to die today.

He mistook the body for the soul. The rich man said to himself, "Take life easy; eat, drink and be merry" (Luke 12:19), but God said, "Your soul is required of you" (v. 20 NASB). This man's perspective on life was from the physical not the spiritual.

We live in a society permeated with an overemphasis on the physical. Marketing strategies from Wall Street to your street and mine appeal to our desires for food, fashions, and the physical appearance of the body at the expense of due consideration for the soul. The sin of greed often works in conjunction with the sin of lust and gluttony. Soon, pride and envy rear their ugly heads. Before long, the sin of greed has multiplied into two or three other sins. The grip becomes as constricting as a boa constrictor that is squeezing the life out of its victim.

Although we are physical beings, we often forget that we are also spiritual beings. Whereas people spend many hours and dollars pampering and exercising their physical bodies, they neglect the spiritual dimension of life. Although I am all for maintaining health and looking good, let us not forget that when we stand before God, he will not ask us how many miles we can jog, if we wear the latest fashions, or if we live in an upscale neighborhood. He will ask us about our spiritual relationship with him. What will be required? Our soul.

He mistook what was God's for what was his. The rich man said to himself, "You have plenty of good things laid up" (Luke 12:19). But God asked, "Who will get what you have prepared for yourself?" (v. 20).

We all have heard the ultimate wisdom concerning wealth: "You can't take it with you." I have never seen a hearse pulling a U-Haul. The oft-asked question concerning the wealthy is, "How much did he leave behind?" The only appropriate answer to that question is, "Everything!"

At the heart of this third error is the confusion between ownership and stewardship. All that we are and all that we have belong to God. Nothing is ours to own; it is ours only on loan. Our responsibility on earth is to manage what is rightfully God's.

Consequently, we must hold everything loosely. Corrie ten Boom, the Dutch lady who was imprisoned at Auschwitz for harboring Jews during World War II, used to say in broken English, "I have learned that I must hold everything loosely because when I grip it tightly, it hurts when the Father pries my fingers loose and takes it from me!"

A Final Warning

Jesus ended his parable with another warning: "This is how it will be with anyone who stores up things for himself but is not rich toward God" (Luke 12:21). Jesus seems to have contrasted two types of people: those who store up things for themselves, who are caught in the grip of greed, and those who are rich toward God, who have released their grip on greed.

If I read this verse correctly, it seems to be saying that God wants me to be rich—rich toward him.

In the 1950s, the European wrestling champion Yussif the Turk came to America to fight Strangler Lewis for the "world championship" and $5,000. Yussif won and insisted that that $5,000 be paid in gold, which he stuffed into his championship belt. The money mattered so much that he refused to remove the belt until he had reached home safely. Boarding the first available ship to Europe, he headed home. But half way across the Atlantic, the ship foundered in a storm and began to sink. In a panic, Yussif jumped for a lifeboat, missed, and went straight to the bottom. His golden belt had become a golden anchor, a vivid illustration of the deadliness of greed.

The questions that the sin of having more claims to answer can be satisfied only in a personal relationship with Jesus Christ. The satisfaction that greed promises can be met only in an ongoing walk with Jesus Christ. The more consistent I am in pursuing that relationship, the less obsessed I will be with having more.

In the parable, Jesus referred to the rich man as a fool. Although society envied the farmer, Jesus said that he was a fool to be pitied. The term *fool* in biblical language is not a description of mental ability but of spiritual discernment. It is an individual who makes choices as if God doesn't exist and who lives as if God hasn't spoken.

If that description fits us, then we are choked by the grip of greed. And it's no laughing matter. We need to be released from the terror of its stronghold. A change in lifestyle will begin to pry our fingers loose.

Study Questions

1. In what areas of your life are you most unsatisfied, consumed to have more?

2. What "stuff" in your life would you have difficulty letting go of?

3. What are some of the effects of greed on people's lives?

4. What is your reaction to people of more means than you?

5. Jesus said more about money than he did about heaven or hell. Why did he do that?

6. Of the three mistakes that the rich farmer made in Jesus' story—mistaking time for eternity, mistaking the body for the soul, mistaking what is God's for what is his—which do you struggle with the most? Why?

RELEASING THE HOLD

At the age of eighty-five, Nadine Stair wrote the following short essay titled "If I Had My Life to Live Over":

I'd like to make more mistakes next time. I'd relax. I would limber up. I would be sillier than I have been this trip. I would take fewer things seriously. I would take more chances. I would climb more mountains and swim more rivers. I would eat more ice cream and less beans. I would perhaps have more actual troubles, but I'd have fewer imaginary ones.

You see, I'm one of those people who live sensibly and sanely hour after hour, day after day. Oh, I've had my moments, and if I had it to do over again, I'd have more of them. In fact, I'd try to have nothing else. Just moments, one after another, instead of living so many years ahead of each day. I've been one of those people who never goes anywhere without a thermometer, a hot water bottle, a raincoat, and a parachute. If I had to do it again, I would travel lighter than I have.

If I had my life to live over, I would start barefoot earlier in the spring and stay that way later in the fall. I would go to more dances. I would ride more merry-go-rounds. I would pick more daisies.[1]

Relax, limber up, kick off your shoes. Life is not complicated, but we have made it complicated.

Nadine is not alone in her slow-down-and-savor-life perspective. Henry David Thoreau, in his classic work *Walden,* urged, "Our life is frittered away by detail. . . . Simplicity, simplicity, simplicity! I say, let your affairs be as two or three, and not a hundred or a thousand."[2] Robert Browning succinctly declared, "Less is more."[3]

Simplicity has seldom been more needed than it is today. Health requires it. Sanity demands it. Contentment facilitates it. Simplicity is crucial to releasing the grip of greed on one's life. If we find ourselves in the quest for more in our emotional, financial, and time commitments, simplicity is one of the best ways to reestablish equilibrium and to slay the dragon of consumption.

The move to a simpler life is not only a good idea but also a biblical mandate. Paul wrote to the Thessalonians, "Make it your ambition to lead a quiet life" (1 Thess. 4:11). In the next verse he explained why: "so that your daily life may win the respect of outsiders and so that you will not be dependent on anybody" (v. 12). Live simply, Paul says, and the hustling world will notice and respect you for it. Live simply and you won't be so burdened with debt or work that you neglect leading the type of life that is pleasing to God.

How Do We Live Simply?

Living simply is keeping first things first. Keeping first things first is a matter of focusing time, attention, and energy on the most important

---

1. Cited in Duane Elgin, *Voluntary Simplicity* (New York: Quill, 1993), 118–19.
2. Henry David Thoreau, *Walden and Civil Disobedience* (New York: Penguin Books, 1983), 135.
3. John Bartlett and Justin Kaplan, eds., *Bartlett's Familiar Quotations*, 16th ed. (Boston: Little, Brown and Co., 1992), 466.

tasks. When we keep first things first, we do not lose sight of our priorities. The benefit of keeping first things first is that it gives us a sense of order in what we do. Focusing on what matters most helps us feel more satisfied and fulfilled. The downside to this approach is that because many people haven't thought through their priorities, they find it hard to figure out what is the most important thing to do first.

Jesus Christ stated clearly our real priority: "Seek first his kingdom and his righteousness, and all these things will be given to you as well" (Matt. 6:33). When we seek God's reign and rule in our lives first, everything necessary will fall into its proper order. Everything hinges upon keeping the "first" thing as first. When we state a magnificent "yes" to God's reign and rule in our lives, we will have the courage to say "no" to secondary pursuits.

Living simply results in a lifestyle adjustment.

Our priorities influence our values. All of us—parents, students, business people, gang members, police officers, and burglars alike—are driven by what we value. Our values reflect that to which we give our lives. Our use of time and our expenditure of energy reflect what is important to us.

A fisherman was sitting lazily beside his boat when a well-dressed businessman came upon him. The businessman was disturbed that the fisherman was lying idly on the bank. He asked why he was not out in the river catching fish.

The fisherman said, "I've caught enough fish for today."

The businessman said, "Why don't you catch more fish than you need?"

"Why would I want to do that?" asked the fisherman.

"You could make more money, buy a bigger boat, go deeper, and catch even more fish. Pretty soon, you would be rich and have a fleet of boats like me," replied the businessman.

"Then what would I do?" the fisherman asked.

The rich businessman said, "You could sit and enjoy life."

"What do you think I am doing now?" the fisherman replied.

The fisherman's values were reflected in how he used his time. He knew that he was successful, although that success was not apparent to other people. He knew that his success was not measured by how much he owned or how much money he had in the bank but by his sense of inner contentment. Contentment, as the fisherman knew, comes not from how much we make but from learning to be content with what we have. Value is something internal rather than external.

We are not likely to relax, limber up, and enjoy a simpler life unless we have found inner peace, which eliminates the constant struggle to possess more.

Living simply involves getting rid of clutter. Clutter is anything that keeps us from being all that we can be. It's anything that distracts, creates detours in our lives, gets in our way, and makes our lives unnecessarily complicated. Clutter could be too many possessions, unreal expectations, overcommitment, controlling people, or emotional baggage. It has the potential to leave us feeling out of control and victimized.

A president of a large publishing company sought out a world-renowned Zen master. After unloading the tremendous business of his life onto the master without provoking much response, he decided to be quiet for a moment. The Zen master began to pour tea into a beautiful Oriental teacup until it overflowed the cup and spread across the grass mat toward the executive. Bewildered, he asked the Zen master what he was doing. The Zen master replied, "Your life is like the teacup, flowing over. There's no room for anything new. You need to pour out, not take in more."

Simplicity seeks to unclutter our lives. Emotionally, we release our worries, reconcile our friendships, forgive our enemies, and begin anew each day. Materially, instead of possession gluttony, we practice deaccumulation. The writer of Hebrews advised, "Let us throw off everything that hinders and the sin that so easily entangles, and let us run with perseverance the race marked out for us" (Heb. 12:1). Like a long-distance runner, we strip away anything that will impede our progress. When we eliminate the unnecessary, the necessary can come to the forefront of our lives.

What we own has a tendency to own us, so for us to win the battle over greed it's imperative that we deaccumulate. Give things away. Or better yet, don't buy what we don't need. Masses of things that are not needed complicate life. They must be sorted, stored, dusted, repaired, serviced, and resorted *ad nauseam*. Most of us could get rid of half of our possessions without any serious sacrifice. If we got rid of the clutter, we could relax, limber up, and enjoy life a lot more.

Living simply is never simple. No matter how simple making that perfect golf swing or playing that flawless piano concerto looks to the casual observer, they are both the result of much careful preparation and execution. The truly great ones make the difficult look effortless because they have practiced. The same is true with living simply. It doesn't just happen that some people have lives that seem to be easy. Things that are worthwhile are worth working and sacrificing for.

So never equate simple with easy. Simplifying your life will take effort, sacrifice, and conviction.

Saying "no" to a society that wants us to buy now and pay later is difficult. Not to mention, being disciplined in our spending and time use habits. Or, for that matter, being committed to keeping our eyes on Christ and his kingdom rule.

Living simply is freedom. Richard Foster, in his classic *Celebration of Discipline*, writes, "Simplicity is freedom. Duplicity is bondage. Simplicity brings joy and balance. Duplicity brings anxiety and fear."[4] Solomon observed that "God made man simple; man's complex problems are of his own devising" (Eccl. 7:29 JB).

One of the principle advantages of living simply is the life of freedom that accompanies it. A simple life is free from anxiety—about our reputations, our possessions, and our tomorrows. When we are controlled by what is life-giving, we refuse to be controlled by what is destructive.

Simplicity brings with it the freedom to enjoy life. The freedom to be all that God created us to be. The freedom to relax. The freedom to limber up. The freedom to enjoy life. The freedom to break loose from the grip of consumption.

---

4. Richard Foster, *Celebration of Discipline* (San Francisco: Harper & Row, 1978), 69.

Simplicity Is Not Something for Bygone Eras

When I engage in a relationship with Jesus Christ, I put him in his rightful and exalted place in my heart. When he is controlling my heart, it causes me to view my longing for more from a new and different perspective. And from that vantage point, the things that I thought I needed are not that important. In fact, I learn that I can live without many of the things I thought I needed so desperately.

Albert Schweitzer was a medical missionary who died in 1965 at the age of ninety. His standard attire was a white pith helmet, white shirt and pants, and a black tie. He had worn one hat for forty years, the tie for twenty. Told one day that some men owned *dozens* of neckties, Schweitzer remarked, "For one neck?"

I love that. It makes me stop and think. I have twenty-nine ties hanging in my closet, some of which I haven't worn in years, and some of which I will probably never wear again.

When Jesus is in his rightful place, it will prompt me to think of what I have, what I need, and what I could live without. Consequently, I might have to perform some subtracting and simplifying of my life. The way of having enough is by accumulating more and more or by desiring less.

Following are some practical steps.

Find happiness in helping others. Paul wrote, "Command those who are rich in this present world . . . to be generous and willing to share. In this way . . . they may take hold of the life that is truly life" (1 Tim. 6:17–19).

Sometimes, I'm afraid, we think that the American Constitution reads, "Life, liberty, and the purchase of happiness." Happiness is not found in what we get but in what we give. We make a living by what we get; we make a life by what we give. If we want to release the grip of greed, we must start by finding someone to whom or something to which we can give ourselves.

Find importance in knowing God. My value is not found in my net worth, or in the kinds of clothes I wear, or in the car I drive, or in the home in which I live. My value has already been determined by God himself. He said, "Look at the birds of the air; they do not sow or reap or store away in barns, and yet your heavenly Father feeds them. Are you not much more valuable than they?" (Matt. 6:26). In fact, I am of such value to God that he sent his son to this earth to die on a cross for my sins. Release from the grip of greed comes by understanding that our true and lasting value comes from God, not from the things that we own or possess.

Find security in trusting God. "Keep your lives free from the love of money and be content with what you have, because God has said, 'Never will I leave you; never will I forsake you'" (Heb. 13:5). God is saying, "I'm with you, no matter where you are on the status totem pole."

Now let me ask, what would give us greater security: having $500,000 in the bank or knowing that God will always be with us and take care of us? Which scenario is the more dependable? Which is the more lasting?

Find satisfaction in relating with God. I am a relational being, created first to be in relationship with God. Just as my individual hereditary characteristics are imbedded in the structure of my chromosomes, so my relational nature is imbedded in the DNA of my soul. I was made for God, and until I find God, a vacant spot will exist in my soul. I might try to fill that emptiness by acquiring more things, but I need to understand that there will never be enough material things to satisfy the longings of the human soul. And when I desire less stuff, I have more contentment, which, by the way, is the most profitable.

Find peace in giving to God. Would you agree that we live in a culture that's pretty materialistic? Our culture would have us believe the lie that having more will make us happy. The one with the most toys wins. And because we are bombarded with this thinking, it is pretty hard to keep our values right. It's hard sometimes when we see everybody else getting more and more.

The strongest antidote to greed is discovering the joy of giving. The essence of greed is get—get more and more. So every time we give, we break the stronghold of greed on our lives. Giving becomes a spiritual victory. It says, "No, I don't buy into the myth that having more will make me happy, that my self-worth is synonymous with my net worth, or that being generous will impoverish my family."

Whenever we give, there's a spiritual victory. The apostle Paul writes, "Command those who are rich in this present world not to be arrogant, nor to put their hope in wealth, which is so uncertain, but to put their hope in God, who richly provides us with everything for our enjoyment. Command them . . . to be generous and willing to share. In this way they will lay up treasure for themselves . . . they may take hold of the life that is truly life" (1 Tim. 6:17–19). God wants us to *enjoy* our wealth, and he also wants us to *share* our wealth.

A Dose of Reality

Elaine St. James recounts in her book *Inner Simplicity* how her family got an important reality check on what really matters in an unexpected way.

> One night, while we were still living in the big house, a huge firestorm came through our area, and we had to evacuate.
>
> Just before we left the house, we looked around and realized how much of the stuff we'd accumulated we could easily get along without.
>
> That's not to say it wouldn't be a hassle if all our possessions got destroyed, and it's not to say that we wouldn't miss some of them. But we'd gotten to a point where we could enjoy our stuff while we had it, and at the same time we wouldn't be devastated if we lost it. That was a big step toward liberation for us.
>
> As it happened, our house didn't burn down. But we saw the evacuation as a good exercise to go through, not only for the uncluttering we ultimately did to simplify our lives, but for releasing our attachment to possessions and achieving a level of inner contentment.
>
> Look around your house and imagine you have thirty minutes to evacuate, and the only things you can take with you are what you can fit in the back of your car. What would you

take? If you had to start all over again, how would you do it differently?

We don't have to wait for nature to intervene. We can take responsibility for our lives and begin right now, today, to get rid of the things and our attachments to the things that get in the way of our inner peace.

When you get right down to it, it's surprising how little we need to be happy.[5]

So go ahead. Be sillier, eat more ice cream, pick more daisies. Simplify your life. Find your security in God. Share your wealth with others. It is an experience that frees from the grip of greed.

Study Questions

1. What pictures come to your mind when you hear the word *simplicity*?

2. Take a moment to determine the major priorities of your life.

3. Jesus said, "Seek first his kingdom and his righteousness, and all these things will be given to you as well" (Matt. 6:33). Write your reflections on the meaning of that statement.

4. Our use of time and our expenditure of energy reflect what is important to us. What do you spend most of your time doing? What does that say about your values?

5. What freedoms would you experience if you began to live more simply?

6. What steps could you take that would lead you into a deeper relationship of trust and security with God?

---

5. Elaine St. James, *Inner Simplicity* (New York: Hyperion, 1995), 120–21.

The Sin of
Lust

11

THE FATAL ATTRACTION

The restaurant hostess turned quickly to lead the couple to their table by the window. The man standing in front did not miss one movement. His wife, painfully aware of the object of his gaze, jabbed him in the side. He shot back angrily, "I wasn't looking at anything." His remark seemed well rehearsed; perhaps from countless other occasions of being caught stealing looks at attractive women. The couple's hurt and anger betrayed the endless cycle of accusation, defense, guilt, effort, helplessness, and failure often associated with struggles of lust.

Lust is a battle for all of us. Men and women, young and old, Christian and non-Christian, clergy and laity have all struggled with it for generations.

The Picture of Lust

David was king of Israel. He wrote many of the psalms. As a devout Jew, he was a person of faith and character. But one spring night he became careless and curious. "One evening David got up from his bed and walked around on the roof of the palace. From the roof he saw a woman bathing. The woman was very beautiful. . . . She came to him, and he slept with her" (2 Sam. 11:2, 4).

He should have been out with his men fighting a war; instead, he took a stroll on the roof of the palace. And down below he saw a beautiful woman bathing. He glanced, and then he stared.

This is a beautiful woman, he thought. His thoughts were not innocent. He desired her; he craved her. He was alone, and he was lonely. He found out about her. He sent for her. He seduced her. He wanted what he wanted, and being king, of course, he could get it. And he did. Eventually, he had his lover's husband killed to cover up his sin. And, to add to the ugliness of this picture, the baby that she conceived died.

What's wrong with this picture? Let's bring this story into sharper focus so we can understand the true picture of lust.

David was in the wrong place *physically*. "In the spring, at the time when kings go off to war, David sent Joab out with the king's men and the whole Israelite army" (2 Sam. 11:1). He should have been leading his men on the battlefront. Instead, he relaxed at the palace with time on his hands.

David was in the wrong place *relationally*. "David remained in Jerusalem" (2 Sam. 11:1). He was alone. He lacked the emotional support that he needed to keep his hormones in check.

David was in the wrong place *mentally*. "From the roof he saw a woman bathing" (2 Sam. 11:2). He allowed his mind to wander. He was thinking impure thoughts. He lounged, then he lingered, and then he lusted.

David was in the wrong place *spiritually*. "The thing David had done displeased the Lord" (2 Sam. 11:27). He glossed over his disobedience. He covered it up, thinking that if no human knew about it, God wouldn't know about it either.

Lust reaps its greatest havoc on our lives when we are in a tempting place, when our mind is not guarded, when we choose to face life alone, and when we are distant from God spiritually.

An Understanding of Lust

Lust is a craving, a yearning, a longing, and a passion. Lust, according to *The American Heritage Dictionary*, "is a sexual craving, especially when excessive; to have an inordinate desire, especially a sexual desire."[1] Although we most often think of lust as involving sex, it is not limited to that domain. We can lust for power, for a car, for a house, or for children.

Lust always starts in the mind. Adultery starts in the head before it ever reaches the bed. First, Satan gets our attention. Then he engages our feelings, resulting in action. Once something has our attention, then it is easier to get our feelings. And once our feelings are engaged, then it is easier for our actions to follow.

I recently shopped for a new car. Each time I visited a car dealership, the salesperson encouraged me, "Go ahead. Take it for a test drive." He wanted to engage my emotions and my feelings with the smell of the new car and the feel of the drive. And once something or someone has my feelings, then it is easier for my actions to follow. That salesman knew that fact, and Satan knows it, too.

This is what happened to David when he desired Bathsheba. He was out for a walk. He looked. Then he looked again. It has been said, "You can't help the first look, but you can avoid the second look that becomes lust." The woman got David's attention. Then, lust got his feelings. The second look created the desire. And once his feelings kicked in, he was easy prey for temptation.

No temptation appears as temptation, and it always seems to be more alluring than it really is. Satan is an expert at packaging and marketing. Just look at advertisements. Never do you see an inebriated man drinking a beer, or the blackened lungs of a person who has smoked cigarettes for thirty years, or the depression of those who have gotten themselves into insurmountable debt. The bait prevents us from seeing the consequence.

Do you remember a few years ago, before the fall of Communism, when a nineteen-year-old German flew his single-engine Cessna Skyhawk 172 airplane hundreds of miles over Russian territory completely undetected, landing safely right in the middle of Red Square?

---

1. Peter Davies, ed., *The American Heritage Dictionary of the English Language* (New York: Dell Publishing, 1977), 419.

Whereas the world was amazed by this feat, the Communist government reacted by arresting the young man immediately and tossing him into prison. Apparently, the young man was so wrapped up in the challenge of accomplishing this feat that he had scant regard for any possible consequences.

Such is lust. Those who succumb to it neither give thought to the consequences nor consider what might lie ahead. They see simply the thrill of a particular moment's challenge.

Have you noticed that we lust *for* or lust *after?* Lust, then, always involves objects. At its most basic level, it is a preoccupation with the objects of our desire. We lust *after* or *for* something or someone, not *with* something or someone. Lust reduces the other person to a non-person. Lust accepts any partner for a momentary service. It has nothing to give. It has nothing to ask. It reduces everything to a mere object, one to be acquired, and then discarded when it's used up.

Lust treats people the way football players treat a football. They cradle and cuddle the ball. They will risk life and limb to protect the ball when their team has it on offense. But once the football crosses the goal line and they score a touchdown, then they throw, pound, and spin the ball on the ground. Then, the players will dance around and mock it. Finally, they ignore it when the game is over. Its purpose has been served. It was merely an object that they used to accomplish a goal.

If you have been the object of someone's lust, you know how demeaning it feels.

Lust is deadly. *Oh, surely not,* you say. But think about it. From where do promiscuity, rape, incest, pornography, prostitution, adultery, many unhappy marriages, and a lot of divorces come, if not from lust? To add to its destructiveness, it causes bitterness, guilt, disillusionment, and strained relationships. Its consequences are mental, social, vocational, and spiritual heartbreak.

If you have ever heard of how an Eskimo kills a wolf, you know that the process is grisly, yet it offers fresh insight into the stages of lust—its desire, deception, and demeaning and deadly nature.

First, the Eskimo coats his knife blade with animal blood and allows it to freeze. Then he adds another layer of blood, and another, until the blade is completely concealed by frozen blood.

Next, the hunter buries his knife in the ground with the blade up. When a wolf follows his sensitive nose to the source of the scent and discovers the bait, he licks it, tasting the fresh frozen blood. He begins to lick faster, more and more vigorously, lapping the blade until the keen edge is bare. Feverishly now, harder and harder the wolf licks the blade in the arctic night. So great becomes his craving for blood that the wolf does not notice the razor-sharp sting of the naked blade on his own tongue, nor does he recognize the instant at which his insatiable thirst is being satisfied by his own warm blood. His carnivorous appetite just craves more—until the dawn finds him dead in the snow!

Lust desires, deceives, demeans, and eventually destroys just that way.

Putting on the Blinders

So what are we to do to avoid the fatal attraction of lust in our lives? Following are some practical suggestions to keep us away from the deadly attraction of lust.

Minimize the opportunity for temptation. The proper way to guard against lust is to steer away from tempting situations. The person who places himself or herself in less than desirable situations is playing with fire: when he gets too close, he will get burned.

Reduce the odds of lust by controlling the circumstances that lead to lust. "Abstain from all appearance of evil" (1 Thess. 5:22 KJV). When I abstain from evil appearances, I will also abstain from the evil itself. If I take care of how things *look,* I take care of how things *are.*

Monitor your thoughts. A humorist said, "I never let my mind wander; it is too small to be out by itself." The way to keep lust from occurring is to keep our thoughts in line. When we fail to monitor our thoughts, it's easy for them to drift into dangerous territory before we know it.

Given the right circumstances, any person can be attracted to lust. The first step of the fall always begins with the mind. The battle of lust begins and ends in the mind. Granted, your mind is your business. Only you can police your mind, but if you are going to win the battle with lust, you must get serious with your thought life.

Magnify the consequences. For every lustful thought ask yourself, *Is this worth it?* Whether it is an affair, a bigger house, an expensive car, or an ambitious promotion, ask yourself, *If I got it, would it be worth it to me, my family, and my future?*

When we go outside the boundaries of God's laws to accomplish a God-given desire in an ungodly way, we will endure the consequences of disobedience. When we ignore God's laws, we don't break them—they break us. The consequences of disobedience are physical pain, relational stain, mental stress, and spiritual separation.

Lust can be conquered. Unfortunately, we will have to fight it for the remainder of our lives.

Study Questions

1. In what areas of your life does lust have its grip on you?

2. What are some subtle and blatant ways that society promotes lust? Why is lust such a powerful enticement?

3. What does the Bible say about lust and its consequences?

4. What does the statement; "We lust *after* or *for* something or someone, not *with* something or someone," mean to you?

5. Put yourself in Satan's shoes. How does he prevent us from seeing the consequences of lust?

6. How could you minimize the opportunities for lust in your life?

12.

AVOIDING THE
FIRST LOOK

A few years ago, I took a busload of senior high students from Overland Park, Kansas, to Washington, D.C., for a leadership conference. After driving all night and arriving a day early to take in some of the sights around our nation's capitol, we checked into the Washington Hilton. We changed clothes and then got back on the bus to travel down to Mt. Vernon to see George Washington's home. As we pulled out of the parking lot of the hotel, one of the students in the back of the bus hollered up to the front, "Rick, there's smoke coming out of our hotel."

I looked back, and, sure enough, smoke was billowing out of the roof of the hotel. In my ever nonchalant, it-will-work-out way, I said, "Oh, I'm sure it's nothing. Drive on, driver. We'll check it out when we get back."

When we returned to our hotel that afternoon, I discovered that it *was* something. A fire had broken out on one of the floors. For reasons of security and safety, neither we nor any of the other guests staying at the hotel could enter the hotel for the next four days. Each night following the conference, we waited in the conference center for instructions about where we would be lodging that night. We stayed in a different hotel for each of four consecutive nights.

One night we stayed in a hotel that was by far the nicest of them all. As usual, it was approaching midnight by the time we arrived. I found my room quickly and got ready for bed. I had just settled in when a student knocked on the door and called out, "Rick! Cindy! You've got to see this!"

"What?" I asked, wondering what kind of accident had happened.

"Come look out our window!"

Our room faced the courtyard. Some of the students' rooms looked out over a street.

I walked across the hall and looked out the window to see that across the street from this luxury hotel was a corner that prostitutes worked. Ten or twelve prostitutes lined the street—dressed in their seductive, revealing, gaudy, and tasteless clothes—and were waving at cars. Many of them called out to the drivers who came by. Some of them got into cars.

"Look at the boots that one under the street light has on."

"That person was only gone twenty minutes," remarked one of the teenage girls.

"Gross!" replied another.

These women fed on the loneliness, boredom, lust, and insecurity of their customers. The demand for their services did not seem to be waning.

I broke up the party, instructing the students to go to bed. Alone.

Our students got an education on this trip to Washington—an education that I had not planned or encouraged and an education that they never forgot. It was a first for me, too.

For some of those men driving by that night, I'm sure it was a first for them, too. Adrenaline shot through their systems, hormones raced through their bodies, and their nerves were all a-tingle. In one cataclysmic moment, they fell prey to the seductive words and bodies of the prostitutes. They crossed the line. Their lives were forever changed, and not for the good. The deadly dart of lust had scored a perfect hit on their hearts. They could have thwarted it. They could have protected their hearts.

The antithesis of lust is love. When we lust, we use people; when we love, we value our relationships and ourselves. To protect ourselves from the fatal attraction of lust, we should have some defensive measures in place.

Understand the Importance of Love

When Jesus spoke to the disciples regarding the first and second greatest commandment, he explained that "these two commands are pegs; everything in God's Law and the Prophets hangs from them" (Matt. 22:40 *The Message*). To the people of Israel, as well as to many believers today, it would seem more logical for obedience to be the peg from which the Law hangs because the point of writing a law is adherence to it. And it is written, "If you love me, you will obey what I command" (John 14:15). Yet, Jesus also said, "A new commandment I give you: Love one another" (13:34). The apostle Paul goes on to tell us that "love is the fulfillment of the law" (Rom. 13:10).

This point might sound irrelevant to our generation, which depends on guns, force, and police departments, to uphold and fulfill the law. Yet, Jesus' simple command requires greater strength than any of us possesses naturally—more power than that of any man-made weapon.

The logic of Paul's interpretation of Jesus' command that love fulfills the Law seems equally simple. For if one loves his neighbor, he will not commit adultery with his neighbor's spouse. If he loves his coworker, he will not lie to him. If he loves his enemy, he will not slander him. And, if one loves people, they will not become the object of his or her lust. Love fulfills the law because if we truly love every person "because he is a person," we will not desire to hurt or violate him or her and, therefore, will never break the Law. God established love as the impetus for obedience. Love fulfills the Law, thereby providing an impetus for obedience that thwarts the second look of lust.

The Active Nature of Love

Love is a verb. It is active, especially when we seek to avoid the fatal attraction of lust. Following are a few ways by which you can embody love and make it active in your life to protect yourself from the deadly darts of lust.

Immerse yourself in God's Word. Avoiding the second look of lust begins with being a person in love with God's Word. The psalmist asked, "How can a young man keep his way pure?" His conclusion: "By living according to [God's] word" (Ps. 119:9). God's Word sanctifies us. It sets us apart from the rest of the world. It makes us holy, clean, and consecrated for God's higher purposes. It informs and reminds us that sexual fulfillment comes in the context of marriage.

We live in a world that wants us to believe the opposite. Our culture bombards us with words, images, advertisements, movies, television, pictures that sex before marriage is fun, freeing, and fulfilling. It would be easy to get sucked into that lie, to be overwhelmed by culture's onslaught, if we were not people of the Word.

We're all familiar with the saying "Garbage in, garbage out." I propose that the opposite is true, too: purity in, purity out. David wrote of Scripture, "The words of the LORD are flawless, like silver refined in a furnace of clay, purified seven times" (Ps. 12:6). When I immerse my mind and heart in the flawless, purified words of God, the siren song of popular culture begins to sound like what it is: a hideous croak. If we hope to be sexually pure in the midst of a sex-orientated culture, we must replace worldly thinking with God's thoughts as found in his Word. His ideas of right and wrong, his promises, and his teachings must saturate our souls. Regular, consistent exposure to God's Word is an important combatant to the alluring lies of our culture.

Avoid tempting situations. A transport company placed a very important ad in a local newspaper that read, "WANTED: Conscientious and experienced truck driver to transport TNT across narrow mountain roads. Pay is very good." Three brave drivers interviewed for the job. The foreman asked each of them this question: "When you round a curve on a tight mountain road, how close to the edge can you drive without slipping off?"

The first driver responded, "Oh, I've had years of experience at that! I can get as close as a foot from the edge."

The second applicant said, "I can hang the outside edge of my tire over the edge and still stay on the road."

The third man replied, "I respect the load and the danger. I would never get close enough to find out."

Guess who got the job?

Sexual temptation is like transporting TNT; it is dangerous. Some people think that they can play with it and not get hurt. Some people think that they can walk right up to the line and have the will power not to cross over. Some people think that they can handle this explosive, but they lack common sense and sound judgment.

Let's own up to it: we cannot handle certain things, and we should never get close enough to them to find out about them. Certain films, videos, and magazines you and I cannot handle. Certain television shows and late-night channels we have no business watching. Certain Internet sites we should avoid. At certain times, we should not be on the computer. Certain music groups and music videos we should not listen to or watch. Certain people, by their stimulating conversations, weaken us. Certain clothes we should not wear. Certain rooms one should never occupy with a member of the opposite sex.

Granted, we can't avoid all sexual stimuli, but as the adage states, "We can't keep the birds from flying over our heads, but we can keep them from making a nest in our hair."

When it comes to sexual temptation, the Bible is quite clear on the appropriate strategy, and that strategy is to run away. "Flee from sexual immorality" (1 Cor. 6:18). Don't debate it. Don't resist it. Don't see how close to the line you can come. Don't flirt with it. Run—fast and hard—away from it. Love compels us to do so. Rehearse the consequences of lustful actions.

A leader of a Christian organization fell into immorality. Afterward, he was asked, "What could have been done to prevent this?"

He paused for a moment, then said with haunting pain and

precision, "If only I had really known, really thought through, what it would cost me and my family and my Lord, I honestly believe I never would have done it."

A law of physics says that for every action there is an equal and opposite reaction. For every sin there is a consequence. One does not sin in isolation. Sin affects not only the sinner but also the offended one and others. It creates a ripple effect that affects individuals and organizations.

The next time you are tempted to cross the line of lust, rehearse the following possible consequences of your actions.

- *Physically*—you might contract a sexually transmitted disease, perhaps infecting your spouse or future spouse or even causing death. You might cause pregnancy with the accompanying personal and financial implications of having a child.
- *Mentally*—you will relive the experience in your mind repeatedly. It's often said that the mind is like a computer. The one noticeable difference, however, is that a computer's memory can be erased whereas what you experience, especially sexually, is retained for life. Those memories and flashbacks could plague future intimacy with your spouse.
- *Emotionally*—You will venture down a path that might lead to addiction. Psychiatrists and therapists who work with various addictions say that sexual addictions are more powerful than alcohol and drug addictions and have a lower successful transformation rate.
- *Personally*—you might lose your self-respect. You might invoke shame and embarrassment upon yourself. You will create a form of guilt that is difficult to shake. Although God will forgive you, you will find it hard to forgive yourself.
- *Professionally*—you might lose your job. You might forfeit your status. You might waste years of training and experience because of having to change a career as a result of impropriety and immorality.
- *Relationally*—you will destroy your example and credibility

with your family. You will lose the respect and trust of your spouse and family members. You might lose your spouse and your children forever. You might cause shame to your family.

- *Spiritually*—you will grieve the Lord who redeemed you. You will drag his name in the mud. One day, you will have to look Jesus in the face and give an account for your actions.

Periodically reviewing and rehearsing the consequences cuts through the fog of rationalization, filling our hearts with the healthy, motivating fear of God.

The writer of Proverbs asked some pointed questions: "Can a man scoop fire into his lap without his clothes being burned? Can a man walk on hot coals without his feet being scorched?" The obvious answer to both questions is no. And he goes on to emphasize, "So is he who sleeps with another man's wife; no one who touches her will go unpunished" (Prov. 6:27–29). The warning has been issued: when you cross the line into sexual immorality, certain and distinct consequences follow.

Guard your mind. "For as he thinks within himself, so he is" (Prov. 23:7 NASB), states the proverb. Jesus said, "Out of the heart come evil thoughts, murder, adultery, sexual immorality . . ." (Matt. 15:19), and ". . . anyone who looks at a woman lustfully has already committed adultery with her in his heart" (Matt. 5:28). Regardless of outward behavior, the true test of sexual purity is our thought life, that which we allow to enter our minds and on which we choose to dwell.

What we do is extremely important, of course. But what we *think* determines what we *do*. Consequently, the only effective and lasting way to change our behavior is to change our minds.

A large railroad switchyard is in St. Louis. One switch that begins with just the thinnest piece of steel directs a train away from one main track and onto another. If you follow those two tracks, you'll find that one ends in San Francisco and the other in New York.

Our thought life, our mind, is a lot like that switch. The seemingly simple choice of that on which we set our minds can determine the outcome of our sexual purity. Solomon wrote, "Above all else, guard your heart, for it is the wellspring of life" (Prov. 4:23). The doorway to the mind is the eyes and ears, so they must be guarded. For us to guard our minds, we must guard what we see and what we hear. It's that simple.

As a crew-cut Sunday school student, I used to sing with gusto, "O be careful little feet where you go . . . little ears what you hear . . . little eyes what you see . . . little hands what you do." Little did I know then that so much about purity, especially sexual purity, would be about wrestling over what my eyes would see, what my ears would hear, where my feet would go, and what my hands would do.

Value the other person. Let's not confuse Christian love with its modern counterfeits—lust, sentimentality, and gratification. Although love is a wonderful, warm emotion, love is not merely a feeling. In fact, according to the Bible, love is primarily an active interest in the well being of another person. Love acts for the benefit of others. Love is the attitude and action that seeks the highest good of every human.

God loved us not because we had something to offer him, but rather because we mattered to him. "For God so loved the world that he gave his one and only Son, that whoever believes in him shall not perish but have eternal life" (John 3:16). God loved us because we were precious to him. He valued us. He loved us because of our worth.

When we value another person, we give one his or her true worth. Dr. W. A. Criswell, former pastor of First Baptist Church, Dallas, Texas, officiated at a lot of weddings. The nervous groom would always say, "Dr. Criswell, how much do I owe you for this?"

Criswell always smiled, looked at the groom, and said, "Aw, just pay me what she's worth." Dr. Criswell made a lot of money on weddings because at that point, to that man, that bride was of unbelievable value.

In like manner, everyone around us is of incredible value to God. His one and only Son died in their place. Because people matter so much to him, they ought to matter to us. Therefore, we should love them as he loves them.

Study Questions

1. What are the most tempting situations for you?

2. Why do you think the Bible's strategy for sexual temptation is to run away?

3. Put yourself in God's place. What emotions must he feel when you live in sin?

4. Since sin begins in the mind, what are some steps that you could take that would change your mind so as to change your behavior?

5. How is love the antithesis of lust and how is love the solution to the sin of lust?

6. What are ways that you could express value toward other persons so as to prevent you from lusting for them?

THE SIN OF GLUTTONY

13

WHEN CRAVINGS ARE OUT OF CONTROL

Consider the following fictitious conversation between a reporter who was touring the advertising agency that is responsible for marketing the Seven Deadly Sins today.

"This is one of my favorites," said the CEO as he led me across the hall. "I will confess that there have been times when I felt that this was one of our weaker departments, but it has been remarkably successful recently. It was originally called *gula*—"

"Gluttony," I said, as I surveyed the room. It had highly polished black and gray marble floors, and was furnished with mauve booths and black marble tables.

"We offer several options here," the CEO explained. "We still have the old-fashioned debauchery for our traditionally minded clients. But our newer products are really selling."

"Oh good, food," I said cheerfully. "Much of Christian fellowship is centered on sharing food, and even the Eucharist—"

"*Please*—I can't go on if you speak about things that make me squeamish," said the CEO.

He continued.

"Food itself is neutral. It can be used for many purposes. We encourage our clients to focus on food itself, rather than the company they're with, the one who provided it, or other distractions."

"Why do you call this sin?"

"Lifestyle," corrected the CEO. "It is variously called 'gourmet eating,' 'real food interest,' and 'the discriminating eater.' But it's all under the umbrella of the 'good life.'"

He introduced me to a pleasant-looking woman named Alice, who showed me charts about the "good life."

"This, in millions, is the number of Americans who spend more than three hours per day thinking about food," she said. She pointed to a very tall bar on her chart.

She then explained what the three other tall bars meant.

"This bar shows the millions of cookbooks produced and dispersed, this the restaurant meals eaten, and this one the millions of dollars people have spent on diet plans and diet foods. I'm particularly proud of that last statistic. Are you impressed?"

"Yes, especially considering the fact that food doesn't ultimately satisfy any more than lust does," I said.

"That's one of its beauties," said Alice. "You finish stuffing it down, and what have you got—extra weight to lose at some health club or diet center!"[1]

Most of us eat a little more than we should, and then we have a second helping. *We don't want to offend the cooks,* we say to ourselves. We let out our belts a notch or two. And, for goodness sake, we won't even try buttoning our coat. We are obsessed with food, physical looks, and dieting. We, too, have fallen prey to Satan's Marketing Strategy.

Contrary to popular opinion, gluttony is not about overeating on Thanksgiving. Gluttony is not about appearance; it is an attitude. It is

---

1. Mary Ellen Ashcroft, "Seven Deadly Sins?: A Guided Tour Through Satan's Marketing Agency," *Discipleship Journal*, no. 83 (1994): 24.

not about being overweight; it is overindulgence. It is not about recreational eating; it is rampant excess. It is not about too many external effects; it is a lack of internal balance.

Gluttony is misdirected hunger. It is the mad pursuit of the bodily pleasures that never completely satisfy. We connect it with the craving for food and this has been its primary expression. But the person who drinks or smokes too much is as gluttonous as the person who overeats. Not to mention the person who watches television excessively or stays on the computer into the wee hours of the night.

What Makes Gluttony Deadly?

What is so bad with a little gluttony, anyway? It's not one of the bad sins, like adultery or stealing. All that gluttony does is make you soft and huggable. It's the cute sin. So what is the problem?

The problem with gluttony is that it seeks to feed the soul with the body's food. It can cause a person to become so full in their stomach that they lose their appetite for God. It can cause a person to become so enamored in their mind that they lose their thoughts for God. The gluttonous have not only a misdirected hunger but also a misplaced God. They pay homage to their appetites; their conspicuous consumption is their extravagant act of praise. Charles Buck described them thus: "Their kitchen is their shrine, the cook their priest, the table their altar, and their belly their God."[2] They no longer eat to live; they live to eat.

One of the crueler tricks of gluttony is that it exacts painful dues while failing to deliver the promised pleasure. In its clear and seductive way, it imposes the very opposite of what it promised. It makes us prisoners and signs our death sentences.

Raynald III, a fourteenth-century duke in what is now Belgium, was grossly overweight. Raynald was commonly called by his Latin nickname, Crassus, which means "fat."

---

2. Cited in Solomon Schimmel, *The Seven Deadly Sins* (New York: Oxford University Press, 1997), 139.

After a violent quarrel, Raynald's younger brother Edward led a successful revolt against him. Edward captured Raynald but did not kill him. Instead, he built a room around Raynald in the Nieuwkerk castle and promised him that he could regain his title and property as soon as he was able to leave the room.

This would not have been difficult for most people because the room had several windows and a door of near-normal size, and none was locked or barred. The problem was Raynald's size. To regain his freedom, he needed to lose weight. But Edward knew his older brother, and each day he sent a variety of delicious foods. Instead of dieting his way out of prison, Raynald grew fatter.

When Duke Edward was accused of cruelty, he had a ready answer: "My brother is not a prisoner. He may leave when he so wills."

Raynald stayed in that room for ten years and wasn't released until after Edward died in battle. By then, his health was so ruined that he died within a year—a prisoner of his own appetite.[3]

People who are caught within the throes of gluttony know all about the prison walls that it establishes. They want to break free, but they can't. Their appetite is too strong. It demands too much. It must be satisfied.

Gluttony is about gaining power. For a moment, the stomach might, indeed, feel a gratifying dominance. We cannot make other people do right. Friends, neighbors, spouse, and children all may resist our will, but that "French Silk Pie" is going to know who is boss. Ironically, overeating might be an assertion of power, but the classic confession of a glutton is, "I have no willpower."

Gluttony is about control. The dimensions of our lives from family to faith and from finances to the future often seem beyond our control. Life is complicated and fraught with compromises, unmet desires, and hurtful disappointments. But with food we can subdue and conquer as much as we choose. The end result is a loss of control.

Gluttony is about mastery. The nature of gluttony is to consume, but those who feast wantonly become themselves morsels. The evil in

---

3. Thomas Bertram Costain, *The Three Edwards* (Garden City, N.Y.: Doubleday, 1962).

gluttony is to master, but eventually he or she is exposed as a slave. Those who succumb to gluttony experience themselves not as rulers, but as helpless servants.

Gluttony is about devouring. Be it food, drugs, sex, computers, sports, television, shopping, or money, but the final consequence, ironically, is to be devoured. In *The Screwtape Letters,* C. S. Lewis has the senior devil, Screwtape, write to his nephew, Wormwood, "To us a human is primarily food; our aim is the absorption of its will into ours, the increase of our own area of selfhood at its expense. But the obedience which the Enemy [God the Father] demands of men is quite a different thing. . . . We want cattle who can finally become food; He wants servants who can finally become sons. We want to suck in; He wants to give out. We are empty and would be filled; He is full and flows over."[4]

When Wormwood ultimately fails in his mission, Screwtape gloats in a fashion that any glutton would find chilling: "I think they will give you to me now; or a bit of you. Love you? Why, yes. As dainty morsel as ever I grew fat on."[5] Carelessly, the glutton falls into a trap and becomes the devil's prey. Poignantly and graphically, Peter writes, "Your enemy the devil prowls around like a roaring lion looking for someone to devour" (1 Peter 5:8).

Gluttons Anonymous

Mastering gluttony is a tricky task because you can never tell when you have arrived. With most sins, you know whether you have mastered them. The thief knows if he did not steal. The dishonest person knows if she did not lie. The adulterer knows if he did not have the affair. With some sins, not much gray area exists. With gluttony, however, it is almost all gray. You cannot simply swear off eating. You've got to eat, so what do you do?

A woman tried everything to lose weight—diet, exercise, and appetite-suppressing pills. Finally, she found something that worked.

---

4. C. S. Lewis, *The Screwtape Letters* (San Francisco: HarperCollins, 2001), 38–39.
5. Ibid., 171.

She attached to her refrigerator door a 12 x 16-inch picture of a beautiful, thin, shapely woman dressed in a bikini. Every time she was tempted to snack, the picture of what she might become was a powerful deterrent. During the first month, she lost ten pounds—but her husband gained twenty!

The point is that what works for some people does not work for others. Try the following action steps, and see if they will work for you.

Feeding. I know that to tell someone who is caught in the grips of gluttony to eat sounds a little ridiculous. But the glutton needs to be fed, or, more precisely, to be fed by God. From Genesis to Revelation, God is portrayed as a caring Father who feeds his people. Eden was planted with "trees that were pleasing to the eye and good for food" (Gen. 2:9); in the new Jerusalem is "the tree of life, bearing twelve crops of fruit, yielding its fruit every month" (Rev. 22:2). In the Song of Songs, we find the main character singing, "He has taken me to the banquet hall" (2:4). And in Revelation, we hear, "Blessed are those who are invited to the wedding supper of the Lamb!" (19:9). We are to ask God daily, "Give us today our daily bread" (Matt. 6:11).

God feeds us. Safe in his pasture, we will not become food. The one who bids us come to the banquet will not devour us; he promises to feed us. But there is more. He does not feed us with the good things that he has made. He feeds us his very self. It is this other bread that we must learn to eat, not "bread alone" but the Word of God himself. Our whole lives consist of learning what he meant when he said, "I have food to eat that you know nothing about" (John 4:32). Jesus bids us to his feast that binds hungry sinners together and links us to the One who alone can feed our souls.

In Western countries, we don't know what it means to be hungry or thirsty. Or, do we? Perhaps our physical hunger and thirst is but a clue that there is a deeper hunger within our soul that can be satisfied by only God himself. In Third World countries, people are dying of physical starvation. In Western nations, people are dying of emotional starvation. In other words, a spiritual hunger exists that cannot be quenched by physical food. Only Jesus himself can satisfy the hunger pangs of the human soul.

Feasting. Feasting isn't gluttony. Gluttony is self-indulgent; feasting is God-honoring. Gluttony has no perspective; feasting keeps perspective. Gluttony is a solitary act that defeats community; feasting is a social act that enhances community. Gluttony ignores God's bounty; feasting celebrates God's blessings.

When the local church gathers for a banquet or a fellowship, it is not only a social event but also a spiritual event. Feasting is a part of our Christian faith. The people of Israel were always feasting—celebrations of thanksgiving for what God had done. Jesus enjoyed feasting. In fact, Jesus said, "The Son of Man came eating and drinking, and they say, 'Here is a glutton and a drunkard, a friend of tax collectors and "sinners"'" (Matt. 11:19). Jesus was at home at feasts and banquets and parties. It is a good thing to remember that the Christian faith is sociable. When believers come together, they celebrate God's goodness and mercy in their lives. During those times, believers take their eyes off the appetites of the body and the desires of their lives to look at Christ and how they can serve him and his people.

Fasting. You might have noticed that I have said nothing about dieting as a counterattack on gluttony. Dieting is a modern phenomenon about which the Bible says nothing. In fact, dieting as it is known in Western countries can be merely the substitution of one of the Seven Deadly Sins for another of them: forsaking gluttony, for example, we fall into pride. Christians have wrestled for a long time with the temptation to misuse food, but the weapon they used wasn't dieting. It was fasting.

Fasting is mentioned in Scripture more times than even something as important as baptism. Notice Jesus' words at the beginning of Matthew 6:16, "When you fast . . ." By giving us instructions on what to do and what not to do when we fast, Jesus assumes that believers will fast. The Bible defines fasting as a Christian's voluntary abstinence from food for spiritual purposes. Fasting is Christian; fasting by a non-Christian has no eternal value because one's motives and purposes in fasting are to be God centered. Fasting is voluntary in the sense that it is not to be coerced. Fasting is more than just the ultimate crash diet for the body; it is abstinence from food for spiritual purposes. Fasting whets the appetite of the soul in hope of experiencing the grace and wonder of God.

Fasting is a means of practicing the reality that we cannot feed the spirit with the body's food. Jesus said, "Blessed are those who hunger and thirst for righteousness, for they will be filled" (Matt. 5:6). If gluttony is misdirected hunger, then fasting is an expression of hungering and thirsting for spiritual food. Gluttony deadens spiritual hunger and numbs our appetite for soul food; fasting keeps us alive to what Jesus knew: "My food is to do the will of him who sent me" (John 4:34).

A few years ago, *People* interviewed Dolly Parton. She credits her family and faith for her character. "I quote the Bible real good!" she boasted. And instead of psychiatry, she turns to fasting, not to diet but for spiritual reasons. "I'll either fast 7, 14 or 21 days. . . . I don't drink nothing but water and I don't ever say when I'm on a fast—Scripture says you're not supposed to." Dolly insists that she has never made a major decision without fasting and praying first.[6]

Jesus expects us to fast like Dolly Parton. And when we do, we find the contours of our souls. We find who we really are before God.

Focusing. The apostle Paul wrote, "But our citizenship is in heaven. And we eagerly await a Savior from there, the Lord Jesus Christ, who, by the power that enables him to bring everything under his control, will transform our lowly bodies so that they will be like his glorious body" (Phil. 3:20–21). This verse identifies the focus of our desire not on earthly things, but on heavenly things; not on what feeds the stomach, but on what nourishes the soul; not on the negative, but on the positive; and not on what will deform, but on what will transform our bodies.

The object of our focus will determine if we have willpower or, better yet, God's power working in our lives, if we are a servant to food or a servant of Christ, and if we are devoured by Satan or fed by God.

A hunger and a thirsting in our souls exists that food and drink can't fill. When we say "No!" to our appetites and "Yes!" to God, we will discover a nourishment that strengthens and sustains our spirit.

---

6. Dolly Carlisle, "After '9 to 5,' Dolly Parton's Movie Career Has Legs; She Beds Burt Reynolds Next," *People Weekly* 15, no. 2 (19 January 1981): 74.

Study Questions

1. The problem with gluttony is that it seeks to feed the soul with the body's food. How is this fact lived out in your life?

2. How could a skinny person be a glutton?

3. Reflect on the irony that overeating is an assertion of power, but the classic confession of a glutton is, "I have no willpower."

4. Contrast feasting and gluttony. What are the benefits and costs of either?

5. What impact would feeding on God's Word have on your personal battle with gluttony?

6. Reflect on the role of fasting to defeat the demons of gluttony.

14

FINDING THE CONTROLS

In December 1993, a thirty-two-year-old man in Buenos Aires died of overeating. At death, he weighed 660 pounds. Five days before he died, he ate an entire piglet for dinner, which put him in the hospital's intensive care ward. To carry him to the hospital, doctors had to call the town's fire brigade.

Any appetite that's out of control is dangerous, whether it is the appetite for food, sex, money, or power.

Most of us are familiar with the need for self-control. If we are honest with ourselves, we tend to be gluttons out of control. We criticize too much. We gossip too much. We overeat. We overspend. We indulge in bad habits, thinking that one more time won't hurt. Sometimes we simply don't think at all; we react, ignoring our need for self-control. And where has it gotten us? Many people live in debt. A large percentage of the population is overweight and out of shape. Clearly, we struggle to say no to ourselves.

Why can't we get out of debt? Why can't we lose weight? Why can't we get in shape? Why can't we say no to an adulterous lifestyle? We can't because we lack self-control.

The Bible offers some practical guidance on developing self-control. The theme of self-control can be found throughout the Bible, but it especially permeates Peter's epistles. He writes, "Therefore, prepare your minds for action; be self-controlled; set your hope fully on the grace to be given you when Jesus Christ is revealed" (1 Peter 1:13). "The end of all things is near. Therefore be clear minded and self-controlled so that you can pray" (4:7). "Be self-controlled and alert. Your enemy the devil prowls around like a roaring lion looking for someone to devour" (5:8). "For this very reason, make every effort to add to your faith goodness; and to goodness, knowledge; and to knowledge, self-control" (2 Peter 1:5–6). Peter not only talked piously about self-control; he practiced it rigorously.

So should we. No race is won without it. No temptation is overcome without it. No mind is sharpened without it. No defeating habit is mastered without it. No right decision is made without it. No craving is restrained without it.

What Does It Mean to Have Self-Control?

Self-control enables us to stay within God-ordained boundaries. Self-control is the ability to avoid excess and to stay within reasonable boundaries. Throughout Scripture, God has outlined the boundaries or standards for our behavior. Self-control enables us to stay within those boundaries.

I loved to color when I was a child. I still do. At first, my coloring attempts were simply efforts to put the crayons on the paper with little regard for the lines. But as I matured, I learned that to create a beautiful picture, I needed to stay within the bold lines. Finding the controls that help us to avoid the excess of gluttony works the same way. As we mature in the faith, our self-control increases, enabling us to live within God's standards.

When the Bible speaks of self-control, it paints a picture of people who are the masters of themselves. They have their appetites and emotions governed so they can do what pleases God rather than themselves.

Self-control evidences the Holy Spirit's work in us. Self-control is a fruit, or evidence, of the Holy Spirit's work in our lives. How does this work? The Spirit does not *make* us do things; instead, he *enables* us to control ourselves. Many things seek to control us: habits, greed, selfishness, and pride. But when we submit to the rule and reign of the Spirit instead of doing what we are driven to do, we act under control. As the Spirit controls us, we do not do things because we should not do them; we do not do things because the deepest part of us understands where real life is found. When we are controlled by the Spirit, we choose to honor Christ by walking away from those things that displease him and walking toward those things that glorify him. Self-control is more "want to" than "should." The basis for our decision comes from knowing God and desiring to please him. True self-control does not bicker and gripe and badger us with negatives. It is a friend who is at our side, encouraging us with incentives and positive reinforcement. Self-control is self-caring, not self-castigating; therefore, we should cultivate it.

Self-control provides protection. The writer of Proverbs wrote, "Like a city whose walls are broken down is a man who lacks self-control" (Prov. 25:28). The walls of a city were its principal line of protection against an invading army in ancient days; without the walls, the city was vulnerable. It was easy prey for an enemy. Because we are at war with our sinful passions, especially as it relates to our appetites, self-control becomes the wall of defense against the sinful desires that wage war against the soul. Without self-control, we yield to the first assault on our ungoverned passions. We offer no resistance, having no discipline, and temptation becomes the occasion of sin. We succumb to that which we had not contemplated. Our appetite leads to unbridled cravings, which plunge us into gluttony.

Self-control grants freedom. Once the life is under control, a liberating freedom ensues. We are not truly free until we have mastery over ourselves. Only the disciplined person experiences freedom. Often, freedom is defined as *living as one pleases.* In reality, freedom is *behaving as one should.* Self-control liberates by enabling us to perform those activities that are essential and mandatory. Self-control is one of the best friends we can have. It will enable us to become the persons we want to be and to perform the activities we want to do. We should cherish this friend always.

What Needs to Be Controlled?

Every aspect of one's life needs control. Controlled lives are happier and fuller lives. If we are to defeat the demons of gluttony, where do we begin?

Self-control begins with the body.

Self-control for the Christian begins with the body. "Each of you should learn to control his own body in a way that is holy and honorable" (1 Thess. 4:4). The apostle Paul wrote, "I urge you, brothers, in view of God's mercy, to offer your bodies as living sacrifices, holy and pleasing to God—which is your spiritual worship" (Rom. 12:1). Controlling our bodies is a spiritual act.

Elisabeth Elliot wrote in *Discipline: The Glad Surrender,* "More spiritual failure is due, I believe, to this cause than to any other: the failure to recognize this living body as having anything to do with worship or holy sacrifice. Failure here is failure everywhere else."[1] The body is important because it houses the Holy Spirit, who directs our longings to grow in Christlikeness.

Our bodies are for the glory of God. When we understand that every physical activity is a spiritual act, that realization will change the way we live and what we eat.

Self-control is revealed in the way we think. Studies have reported that in certain people, thinking about food increases their insulin level, which makes them feel hungry. Thinking about food doesn't actually add pounds, but it does increase one's appetite.

Our thoughts stimulate our appetites, and appetites can lead to sin. Our mind has tremendous control of one thing: our behavior. Sooner or later, our thoughts lead to our actions. If we do not control them, the consequential actions can be destructive, if not deadly. The apostle Paul wrote, "We take captive every thought to make it obedient to Christ" (2 Cor. 10:5). This means entertaining in our minds only those thoughts that are acceptable to God. Observe the following guideline for controlling our thoughts: "Finally, brothers, whatever is true, whatever is noble, whatever is right, whatever is pure, whatever is lovely,

---

1. Elisabeth Elliot, *Discipline: The Glad Surrender* (Old Tappan, N.J.: Revell, 1982), 45.

whatever is admirable—if anything is excellent or praiseworthy—think about such things" (Phil. 4:8).

Our minds are mental greenhouses where unlawful thoughts, once planted, are nurtured and watered before being transplanted into the real world of unlawful actions. People seldom fall suddenly into gluttony. This sin is savored in the mind long before it's enjoyed in reality. The thought life, then, becomes a major line of defense in the battle of our appetites.

How do we control our thoughts? Solomon gave sound advice when he wrote, "Above all else, guard your heart, for it is the wellspring of life" (Prov. 4:23). In ancient thinking, the heart was the central organ that controlled all activities and so determined the character of living; therefore, we must guard the heart closely because it is the pivotal source and dominating factor of life. The doorway to the heart is the ears and eyes.

Are we careful to control what has the focus of our attention? The psalmist wrote, "I will set no worthless thing before my eyes" (Ps. 101:3 NASB). "Be self-controlled and alert. Your enemy the devil prowls around like a roaring lion looking for someone to devour" (1 Peter 5:8).

How Do We Gain Control?

Gaining control need not be an unattainable mountain summit. Don't lose hope. Help is available. How can we acquire self-control to starve the gluttony monster? No simple, fast formula exists, but some basic elements do. Undergirding all that would lead to self-control is submitting one's life to the leadership of Christ and using the strength and power that is available to us through him.

Know what you want. It is impossible to develop self-control without knowing one's objective. If you want to lose weight, you must know what size you want to be. To break a bad habit, you must know what good habit you want to develop.

Knowing what you want is the starting point of discipline. Solomon wrote, "Where there is no vision, the people are unrestrained" (Prov. 29:18 NASB). The word *unrestrained* denotes the picture of an unbridled horse. It runs wild. It is out of control. People without direction are purposeless. They waste their energy on less important things because they lack self-control.

Say no to the lesser things to say yes to the greater things. Self-control is always a matter of choice. Mastery of our appetites cannot be legislated or forced upon us. It does not happen because someone demands it of us; it comes as the result of right choices. And only we can make those choices.

Choosing what is right mandates an ability to say no to many cravings and urges. But when we say no to the inappropriate concerns, we can say yes to what matters most.

Perform the hard part first. This is the principle of delayed gratification. M. Scott Peck described delayed gratification as "a process of scheduling the pain and the pleasure of life in such a way as to enhance the pleasure by meeting and experiencing the pain first and getting it over with." He adds, "It is the only decent way to live."[2]

Often, at first, we cannot see the fruits of delayed gratification, but if we live believing in and practicing self-control, they will become visible. Presently, all we might see are the unwanted pounds, the flabby muscles, or a defeating habit, but if we wait, resolutely performing the hard part first, the desired result eventually will be a reality. The payoff is worth the wait.

Be purposeful in everything you do. By following this principle, we become intentional in everything we do. We are constantly asking ourselves, "Will this activity help me reach my final destination? Does this pursuit enhance the priorities I have established?"

Depend on Christ's strength. If we want to develop self-control, we must learn to depend on Christ's power to help us. The most accurate and descriptive term for self-control is "Christ control." Self-control is not merely a self-produced behavior. "For God did not give us a spirit of timidity, but a spirit of power, of love and of self-discipline" (2 Tim. 1:7). God becomes the soul-stirring dynamic that enables us to counter the assault of gluttony.

When we yield our desires and passions to the Master, he provides

---

2. M. Scott Peck, *The Road Less Traveled* (New York: Simon and Schuster, 1978), 18.

the inner dynamic to help us defeat these urges. The mastery of our life can occur only with God at the helm. "Let the Spirit direct your lives, and you will not satisfy the desires of the human nature" (Gal. 5:16 GNB). God's unlimited power provides the needed strength to control our lives. We can try all we want, but we have not used all of the strength that is available to believers until we draw upon the Lord— the source of all strength.

A young boy was helping his father bring in some wood for the fire, and he was struggling under the weight of a heavy load. "Why don't you use all of your strength?" the father asked.

"I am," the lad responded, feeling dejected.

"No you're not," declared the father. "You have not asked me to help you." The father reached down and lifted both the boy and the log in his arms. When we cast our burdens on the Lord, he will sustain us.

Self-control has our best interests at heart. People who exercise self-control are happier and healthier because they are fulfilling their inner potential. Self-control is one of the best friends we could have. Many people never learn the joy of self-control; consequently, they never control the cravings and fall prey to deadly sins such as gluttony.

Study Questions

1. What areas of your life are prone to being out of control?

2. What does it mean to have self-control?

3. In what ways would a more controlled life offer you protection and grant you freedom?

4. Since your mind has tremendous control over your behavior, what steps do you need to take to bring your mind under control?

5. Do you need to let Christ take control of your life? Consider what you need to do so that Christ is in full control.

Epilogue

I have a confession to make. I hate writing about sin. I'm against sin, mind you. And I do preach against it in my church. But most people who read my books and listen to my sermons don't need to be convinced that they are sinners; they already know it.

But sometimes I think that people forget the dangerous and deadly consequences of sinful behavior. It's like sitting in a chair looking directly into the barrel of a loaded gun that is set on a timer to fire at an undetermined moment within the next ten years. Too often, we gamble that the loaded consequences of sin will not happen to us. But it does. Look around at the people you know who have fallen prey to the dangerous consequences of sin. No one is immune. No one is safe.

My hope is that this book has been a wake-up call regarding the deadly consequences of sin. My hope is that you have walked away from our time together refusing to sit in the chair with a loaded gun set to go off. My hope is that you will be mindful of the damage, both temporal and eternal, of living in sin. Furthermore, my hope is that you have learned some positive countermeasures to avoid sitting in the dangerous chair of sin. My hope is that you will put into action the steps to avoid the danger. If that has happened, our time has been well spent.